9ᵗʰ Sound and Music Computing Conference

Illusions

11-14 July 2012
Aalborg University Copenhagen

Conference Guide

Bibliographic information published by the Deutsche Nationalbibliothek

The Deutsche Nationalbibliothek lists this publication in the Deutsche
Nationalbibliografie; detailed bibliographic data are available
in the Internet at http://dnb.d-nb.de .

ISBN 978-3-8325-3180-5

Logos Verlag Berlin GmbH
Comeniushof, Gubener Str. 47,
10243 Berlin
Tel.: +49 (0)30 42 85 10 90
Fax: +49 (0)30 42 85 10 92
INTERNET: http://www.logos-verlag.de

SMC 2012

9th Sound and Music Computing Conference

11–14 July 2012, Aalborg University Copenhagen

Organized by

With the support of the Culture Programme of the European Union

Culture · Education and Culture DG

Culture Programme

Institutional partners

DANSK KOMPONIST FORENING

FONDEN FOR ENTREPRENØRSKAB
YOUNG ENTERPRISE DANMARK

Danish Sound Technology Network

Digital Re-working/
Re-appropriation of
Electro-Acoustic Music

TABLE OF CONTENTS

WELCOME

It is our pleasure to welcome you all to the 9th edition of the Sound and Music Computing Conference taking place in Copenhagen. We are happy to be able to host you at Aalborg University's new facilities in Copenhagen South Harbour, where Aalborg University Copenhagen has moved from July 1st. We are also excited about the collaboration with several art galleries and exhibition spaces in the center of Copenhagen, where the main musical events will take place.

A summer School takes place just before the conference, with about 40 PhD and Master students attending lectures and working on projects around the topic of product sound design, innovation and entrepreneurship. We are welcoming Cumhur Erkut, Andy Farnell and Davide Rocchesso as main teachers at the summer school, sharing their expertise in interactive procedural sound and interaction. We are also happy that Søren Bech, head of research at Bang and Olufsen and Veronique Larcher, head of research of Sennheiser for North America, are talking at the school.

The scientific program of the Sound and Music Computing Conference should present a palette of contemporary work rich with new ideas and reflective on old.

We are excited to welcome three keynote speakers: Professor Michael Kubovy from the University of Virginia presenting his work on audio-visual objects, Esben Skovenborg from TC Electronic talking about current challenges to good sound quality and Professor Lars Kai Hansen from Danish Technical University talking about cognitive components of audio spaces.

This year, we received 142 submissions, and accepted 78. All sound and music computing topics were selected by authors to describe their work, but the most popular topics include: interfaces for sound and music (38), interactive performance systems (36), automatic music generation and accompaniment systems (25), perception and cognition of sound and music (20), and models for sound analysis and systems (20). Among the papers we accepted, the topics are: interfaces for sound and music (13), interactive performance systems (13), computer environments for sound and music processing (9), automatic music generation and accompaniment systems (8), music information retrieval (8), and sound and music signal processing algorithms (7). Countries with the highest number of authors on submissions include: Japan (31), UK (28), France (24), USA (23), Italy (21), Canada (17), Austria (13). We wish to thank the technical program committee for their work in facilitating the review process, and guiding the selection process with helpful summaries of reviews submitted by 130 reviewers. We also wish to thank all reviewers for their thoughtful critiques of each paper, which ensured that over 84% of the papers received 3 independent and helpful reviews.

We received the unprecedented 123 music submissions, representing the creators from 5 different continents. Juraj Kojs, the Music Programme Chair led the team of 6 curators (Scott Barton, Paula Matthusen, Chikashi Miyama, Steven Kemper, Troy Rogers and Spencer Topel) in the discussion on the artistic and technical qualities of the submissions. Together with the invited composers' pieces and works by the curators, the final program consists of 31 works. This year's special edition also features the invited composer Judith Shatin who has championed the world of electroacoustic music around the globe.

Out of 61 submissions for the electro-acoustic music concert, Spencer Topel molded an intriguing program of 9 compositions. The concert is presented by the Figura Ensemble, the premier Copenhagen-based new music group. Music of J. Shatin and invited Danish work by Jesper Holmen are scheduled for this opening concert. In the category of new music instruments and interfaces, we received 24 submissions. For Concert 2, Chikashi Miyama created a 6-piece program, including iPhones, swarming robotics, a typewriter and homemade instruments. Expressive Machines Musical Instruments received 9 proposals for new works with their CARI, AMI and TAPI robotic instruments. In close collaboration between EMMI and the composers, 5 selected proposals were transformed into full-fledged works. Judith Shatin's Sic Transit is also presented on the concert. We received 29 submissions in the category of sound installations. Paula Matthusen sculpted a 6-work program that engages test tubes, stretched canvas, open fire, surgery table, windows and constructed domes. The installations showcase fascinating environments for listening experiences.

In an effort to engage the community with the conference, the three concerts are scheduled in the Copenhagen's venues Den Frie and Overgaden. Likewise, the installations are on the view at the city's Black Box Gallery and Damp Gallery in addition to those at the Medialogy Aalborg University Copenhagen site. All in all, the music program for this year's conference is widely diverse in its musical ambition and technology involvement. We believe that it represents a healthy sample of the current trends in the domains of electronic music and multidisciplinary sound.

We would like to thank all our sponsors who have made this event possible. In particular, the Danish Sound Technology Network that has supported the travel of our keynote speakers, the Danish Art Council that has covered travel expenses for our curators, the danish Composers' Society's Production Pool that has supported one musical event and the Culture Programme of the European Union that has supported refreshments and catering. We would also acknowledge the generous support of young enterprise Denmark that has made the summer school possible. Finally, we would like to thank all our colleagues and students' helpers that with their hard work have made this event possible.

Overall, we have been very busy preparing for you an event which will hopefully be a stimulating learning experience, where you will also have time to explore our city while appreciating different events. We hope you will enjoy the possibility to be surrounded by inspiring research and captivating music, and we welcome you to wonderful Copenhagen!

Stefania Serafin, General Chair
Bob L. Sturm, Sofia Dahl and Jan Larsen, Scientific Programme Chairs
Juraj Kojs, Music Programme Chair
Rolf Nordahl, Summer School Chair

SCIENTIFIC COMMITTEE

General Chair
Stefania Serafin (Aalborg University Copenhagen, Denmark)

Scientific Programme Chairs
Bob L. Sturm (Aalborg University Copenhagen, Denmark)
Sofia Dahl (Aalborg University Copenhagen, Denmark)
Jan Larsen (Technical University of Denmark, Denmark)

Music Programme Chair
Juraj Kojs (Ai Miami International University of Art & Design, USA)

Summer School Chair
Rolf Nordahl (Aalborg University Copenhagen, Denmark)

Local Organizing Committee at Aalborg University Copenhagen
Niels Böttcher, Sofia Dahl, Steven Gelineck, Niels C. Nilsson, Rolf Nordahl, Jon Ram Bruun-Pedersen, Stefania Serafin, Erik Sikström, Eva Sjuve, Bob L. Sturm, Stefano Trento, Rebecca Engberg (Technical University of Denmark, Denmark)

Scientific Committee
Mads Christensen (Aalborg University, Denmark)
Bruno Giordano (McGill University, CA)
Federico Fontana (University of Udine, Italy)
Nick Collins (University of Sussex, UK)
Simon Dixon (Queen Mary University of London, UK)
David Meredith (Aalborg University, Denmark)
Federico Avanzini (University of Padova, Italy)
Agnieszka Roginska (New York University, USA)
Dan Overholt (Aalborg University Copenhagen, Denmark)
Juan Bello (New York University, USA)

Davide Rocchesso (IUAV, Italy)

Gualtiero Volpe (University of Genova, Italy)

Alexander Jensenius (University of Oslo, Norway)

Roberto Bresin (KTH, Sweden)

Fabien Gouyon (INESC Porto, Portugal)

Laurent Daudet (University Paris VII, France)

Mark Grimshaw (Aalborg University, Denmark)

Jeff Snyder (Princeton University, USA)

Music Committee

Scott Barton (University of Virginia, USA)

Steven Kemper (University of Virginia, USA)

Paula Matthusen (Wesleyan University, USA)

Chikashi Miyama (ZKM, Germany)

Troy Rogers (University of Virginia, USA)

Spencer Topel (Dartmouth College, USA)

Reviewers

Domenico Vicinanza, Myriam Desainte-Catherine, Huseyin Hacihabiboglu, Maarten Grachten, Tapio Lokki, Stefano Delle Monache, Perfecto Herrera, Pierre Hanna, Massimo Grassi, David Pirrò, Karin Petrini, Sylvain Le Groux, Sergio Canazza, Carlos Guedes, Hanna Lukashevich, Anders Askenfelt, Anders Friberg, Augusto Sarti, Emilia Gomez, Brian Gygi, João Lobato Oliveira, Eva Sjuve, Jussi Pekonen, F. Amílcar Cardoso, Luis Teixeira, Matija Marolt, Andreas Arzt, Luis Gustavo Martins, Davide Andrea Mauro, Simone Spagnol, Massimiliano Zanoni, Stefan Weinzierl, Alvaro Barbosa, Sylvain Marchand, Sandra Pauletto, Sergi Jorda, Edgar Berdahl, Carlos Pérez-Sancho, Pietro Polotti, Thomas Grill, Emmanouil Benetos, Luca Turchet, Peter Knees, Pierre Jouvelot, Niels Boettcher, Julian Parker, Dominique Fober, Stephen Mcadams, Karmen Franinovic, Piotr Holonowicz, Markus Schedl, Alfonso Perez, Kjetil Falkenberg Hansen, Tillman Weyde, George Tzanetakis, Filipe Cunha Monteiro Lopes, Rui Pedro Paiva, Julius Smith, Stephen Barrass, Haruhiro Katayose, Tomoyasu Nakano, Olivier Lartillot, Laurent Pottier, Carlo Drioli, Véronique Sebastien, Justin Salamon, Shawn Trail, Stefano Zambon, Matthew Davies, Arthur Flexer, Emilios Cambouropoulos, Leon Van Noorden, Steven Gelineck, Antti Jylhä, Stefano Papetti, Fionntán O'Donnell, Tapio Takala, Werner Goebl, John Dack, Giovanni De Poli, Kjartan Olafsson, Steffen Lepa, Dmitry Bogdanov, Cumhur Erkut, Mitsuyo Hashida, Stefan Kersten, Daniel Gaertner, Katy Noland, Bernhard Niedermayer, Balázs Bank, Kazuyoshi Yoshii, Rebecca Fiebrink, Cameron Britt, Gerhard Widmer, Sebastian Flossmann, Andrew Mcpherson, Erik Sikstrøm, Karim Barkati, Daniel Hug, Anastasia Georgaki, Joan Serrà, Matthias Mauch, Christopher Harte, Mari Tervaniemi, Giovanna Varni, Mark Plumbley, Rosemary Fitzgerald, Erwin Schoonderwaldt, Alois Sontacchi, Tamara Smyth, Malcolm Slaney, Christopher Salter, Frederic Bevilacqua, Dirk Moelants, Phillip Stearns, Thibault Langlois, Pedro J. Ponce De León, Matthias Rath, Jordi Janer, Gerard Roma, Mohamed Sordo, Esteban Maestre, Rafael Ramirez.

07-11ᵀᴴ July: Summer School

Product sound design, innovation and entrepreneurship

Future products will rely on our natural capabilities of continuous and physical interaction. Moreover, for the best experience in their use, they need to stimulate, but not saturate, all our senses. Our sense of hearing is quite advanced; yet only a few product developers, engineers, marketing teams, and designers know how to make use of it properly. Our mission in this summer school is to educate the future product design and development team members with a specific competence on interactive sound. The summer school follows up from the Product Sound Design Summer School 2010 (Aalto University, Design Factory, Finland) supported by the COST Action IC0601 Sonic Interaction Design.

Lecture 1: Sonic Interaction Design - *Davide Rocchesso* (University of Venice, Italy)
Human-object and human-human interactions are often facilitated by computational means. Interaction designers aim at designing such interactions to make them more effective and pleasant. Sonic Interaction Design emphasizes the role of sound as a mediator of meaningful interactions.

Lecture 2: Product Sound Design (PSD) Overview - *Cumhur Erkut* (Helsinki University of Technology, Finland)
This introductory lecture provides an overview of the 2010 PSD Summer School at the Aalto Design Factory. It highlights the general process of PSD and introduces the modules that will be practiced in the hands-on session.

Hands on: Puredata – Zero to Hero - *Andy Farnell*

Lecture 3 and 5: Procedural sound - *Andy Farnell*
Andy Farnell will be presenting lectures and workshops where students can understand and create sound effects starting from nothing.
Approaching sound as a process, rather than as data is the essence of Procedural Sound which has applications in video games, film, animation, and media in which sound is part of an interactive process creating a living sound effect that runs as computer code, changing in real time according to unpredictable events. We will use the Pure Data (Pd) language to construct sound objects, which are more flexible and useful than recordings. Participants should come with Pure Data (Extended version) already installed on their laptops, a fully charged battery and a set of headphones.

Lecture 4: Physical Sonic Interactions - *Davide Rocchesso* (University of Venice, Italy)
Physical computing aims at building objects that interact with the analog world by means of digital technologies. Sound synthesis by physics-based modeling provides direct links between the real and the virtual in sonic interaction design. The designer can exploit a combination of physical computing and physics-based sound modeling to sketch physical prototypes of sounding objects.

Lecture 6: Perceptual audio evaluation - *Søren Bech* (Head of research, Bang and Olufsen, Denmark)
The aim of this tutorial is to provide an overview of perceptual evaluation of audio through listening tests, based on good practices in the audio and affiliated industries. The tutorial is geared to anyone interested in the evaluation of audio quality and will provide a highly condensed overview of all aspects of performing listening tests in a robust manner.
Topics will include:
1) Definition of a suitable research question and associated hypothesis;
2) Definition of the question to be answered by the subject;
3) Scaling of the subjective response;
4) Control of experimental variables such as choice of signal, reproduction system, listening room, and selection of test subjects;
5) Statistical planning of the experiments; and
6) Statistical analysis of the subjective responses.
The tutorial will include both theory and practical examples including discussion of the recommendations of relevant international standards (IEC, ITU, ISO). The presentation will be made available to attendees and an extended version will be available in the form of the text Perceptual Audio Evaluation, authored by Søren Bech and Nick Zacharov.

Lecture 7: Product Sound Design Practice - *Cumhur Erkut* (Helsinki University of Technology, Finland)
As a structured process and by hands-on work, we consider how to identify sound-mediated interactions, how to apply the functional, informational, and aesthetic qualities of sound in products groups, and especially how to communicate, sketch, and prototyping sound ideas.

Workshops and Tutorials

Wednesday, July 11ᵀᴴ, 2012

1) Musical Interaction Design with the CUI32Stem: Wireless Options and the GROVE system for prototyping new interfaces
by Dan Overholt, Aalborg University Copenhagen (Half day tutorial, afternoon)

A system for Do-It-Yourself (DIY) interface designs focused on sound and music computing has been developed. The system is based on the Create USB Interface (CUI), which is an open source microcontroller prototyping board together with the GROVE system of interchangeable transducers. Together, these provide a malleable and fluid prototyping process of 'Sketching in Hardware' for both music and non-music interaction design ideas. The most recent version of the board is the CUI32Stem, which is designed specifically to work hand- in-hand with the GROVE elements produced by Seeed Studio, Inc. GROVE includes a growing collection of open source sensors and actuators that utilize simple 4-wire cables to connect to the CUI32Stem. The CUI32Stem itself utilizes a high-performance Microchip® PIC32 microcontroller, allowing a wide range of programmable interactions. The development of this system and its use in sound and music interaction design is described. Typical use scenarios for the system may pair the CUI32Stem with a smartphone, a normal computer, and one or more GROVE elements via wired or wireless connections.

For more information, please see:
http://www.seeedstudio.com/wiki/CUI32Stem

2) Parametric Pitch Estimators for Music Signals - Half day tutorial
by Mads G. Christensen

Many signals produced by musical instruments are approximately periodic or contain periodic components. Such signals can be decomposed into sets of sinusoids having frequencies that are integer multiples of a fundamental frequency. The problem of finding such fundamental frequencies, a task which is often referred to as pitch estimation, is important in many music applications and devices, like in guitar tuners, automatic transcription, and intelligent pitch shifters. In this tutorial, recent advances in parametric pitch estimation are presented. More specifically, a number of new pitch estimators for both single- and multi-pitch signals are presented and their application to music signals discussed. The methods are based on the principles of maximum likelihood estimation, optimal filtering, and subspace methods. The estimators are compared in terms of computational and statistical efficiency and robustness, and open issues and directions for future research are discussed.

3) Sound design for games – Half day tutorial
by Mark Grimshaw

4) Learning Similarity Measures for Music – All day tutorial
by Sebastian Stober

Musical similarity is a central issue in Music Information Retrieval (MIR) and the key to many applications. In the classical retrieval scenario, similarity is used as an estimate for relevance to rank a list of songs or melodies. Further applications comprise the sorting and organization of music collections by grouping similar music pieces or generating maps for collection overview. Finally, music recommender systems that follow the popular "find me more like..."-idea often employ a similarity-based strategy as well.

However, music similarity is not a simple concept. For a comparison of music pieces, many interrelated features and facets can be considered. Their individual importance and how they should be combined depends very much on the user and his specific retrieval task. Users of MIR systems may have a varying (musical) background and experience music in different ways. Consequently, when comparing musical pieces with each other, opinions may diverge. A musician, for instance, might especially look after structures, harmonics or instrumentation (possibly paying – conscious- or unconsciously – special attention to his own instrument). Non-musicians will perhaps focus more on overall timbre or general mood. Others, in turn, may have a high interest in the lyrics as long as they are able to understand the particular language. Apart from considering individual users, similarity measures also should be tailored for their specific retrieval task to improve the performance of the retrieval system. For instance, when looking for cover versions of a song, the timbre may be less interesting than the lyrics.

In order to support individual user perspectives and different retrieval tasks, music similarity should no longer be considered as a static element of MIR systems. Therefore, this tutorial aims to introduce MIR researchers and developers to a variety of existing techniques, which allow them to build systems including an adaptable model of music similarity. We show how to model the task of finding a suitable music similarity measure as a machine learning problem, introduce various learning algorithms, and give examples of interactive applications. The tutorial addresses a broad audience and in particular does not require prior knowledge in machine learning as a prerequisite. The ideas and algorithms covered will be presented up to the level of understanding that enables the audience to successfully apply them.

5) Workshop by EMMI (Expressive Machines Musical Instruments)

A preview of the techniques and technologies used in the robot concert of July 15th.

TECHNICAL PROGRAM

Wednesday, July 11th, 2012 **Registration** 08.00 - 09.00 AM.
Thursday, July 12th, 2012 **Registration** 08.00 - 09.00 AM.
Thursday, July 12th, 2012 **Conference opening and welcome** at 09.00 AM

KEYNOTE ADDRESSES

Keynote Addresses take place in the Auditorium.

Keynote 1:
09.00h – Thursday, July 12th, 2012
Chair: *Stefania Serafin*

AUDIO-VISUAL OBJECTS.
Professor Michael Kubovy, University of Virginia.
In this talk I offer a theory of cross-modal objects. I will discuss two kinds of linkages between vision and audition. The first is a duality. The visual system detects and identifies surfaces; the auditory system detects and identifies sources. Surfaces are illuminated by sources of light; sound is reflected off surfaces. However, the visual system discounts sources and the auditory system discounts surfaces. These and similar considerations lead to the Theory of Indispensable Attributes that states the conditions for the formation of gestalts in the two modalities. The second linkage involves the formation of audiovisual objects, integrated cross-modal experiences. I describe research that reveals the role of cross-modal causality in the formation of such objects. These experiments use the canonical example of a causal link between vision and audition: a visible impact that causes a percussive sound.

Professor Michael Kubovy Cognitive psychologist Michael Kubovy's research focuses on visual and auditory perception, especially perceptual organization; cross-modal perception; and the psychology of art. The latter is the focus of his book The Psychology of Perspective and Renaissance Art. Kubovy's work is widely published in journals such as The Proceedings of the US Academy of Sciences and Experimental Brain Research. His research is currently supported by NSF, with previous awards from NIMH, the National Eye Institute, and the National Institute for Deafness and Communicative Disorders. He has received numerous awards for his achievements, including Cattell and Guggenheim fellowships, election to the select (200 or so members) Society of Experimental Psychologists, and a fellowship at the Rockefeller Center in Bellagio. Among his invited lectures are the Wertheimer Lecture in Frankfurt and the Kanisza Lecture in Trieste, as well as numerous keynote conference addresses. Kubovy received the PhD from the Hebrew University, where he worked with Daniel Kahneman and Amos Tversky. He has held faculty positions at Yale, Rutgers and the University of Virginia.

Keynote 2:
09.00h – Friday, July 13th, 2012
Chair: *Stefania Serafin*

CURRENT CHALLENGES TO GOOD SOUND QUALITY.
Esben Skovenborg, TC Electronic.
Why are many recent CDs so loud? What is the Loudness War, how does it affect music and broadcast programmes - and what is being done to stop it? Why does 'digital' sometimes sound bad? What can you do to maintain good sound quality?
The technical possibilities for achieving great sound quality have never been better than today. Yet many music and broadcast productions seem to suffer from several characteristic problems. This talk will present some of the underlying issues, demonstrate what each one sounds like, and how the relevant audio properties can be measured and controlled.

Esben Skovenborg received the Industrial PhD degree from Aarhus University (Computer science) in 2004, with the topic Measuring Perceptual Features of Music. He also holds an MSc degree in Music Technology from The University of York. Esben has studied music at the Musicians Institute in California, and enjoys playing the guitar. Since 2005 Esben Skovenborg has been employed as a research engineer at TC Electronic A/S, where he works with virtual prototyping, algorithm development, signal processing, software architecture, pattern recognition, and listening experiments. Esben has published a number of papers at AES and DAFx conferences, and has contributed to the international standardisation of loudness-measurement and -control within the ITU-R and the EBU.

Keynote 3:
09.00h – Saturday, July 14th, 2012
Chair: *Stefania Serafin*

THE COGNITIVE COMPONENTS OF AUDIO SPACES.
Professor Lars Kai Hansen, Technical University of Denmark (DTU).
The cognitive component hypothesis is concerned with mechanisms that allow the human brain to solve complex perceptual and cognitive tasks. It is an example of the so-called 'rational' approach to cognitive modeling which focuses on the statistical properties of the brain and the computational challenges that face it in a given environment. The cognitive component hypothesis emphasizes the important role of conditional independence, enabling the brain to simplify computations and focus attention only on relevant dimensions of given environment. I will describe the supervised and unsupervised machine learning methods we have used to design test protocols for the cognitive component hypothesis. The approach is illustrated by examples ranging from modeling of low level properties of speech and music signals, to understanding of high-level aspects of human cognition involved in social behaviors and music organization.

Professor Lars Kai Hansen received the PhD degree in physics from University of Copenhagen, in 1986. He worked on industrial machine learning from 1987-1990, with Andrex Radiation Products A/S. Since 1990 he has been with the Technical University of Denmark, currently he is head of DTU Informatic's Section for Cognitive Systems. Lars Kai Hansen is author/co-author of more than 250 papers and book chapters on adaptive signal processing and machine learning and applications in bio-medicine and digital media.

Oral Sessions take place in the Auditorium.

Oral Session 1: PERCEPTION, COGNITION AND ILLUSIONS
11.00h – 12.20h, Thursday, July 12th, 2012
Chair: *Alexander Refsum Jensenius*

11.00h: [OS1-1] FROM THE SHEPARD TONE TO THE PERPETUAL MELODY AU-DITORY ILLUSION.
Pedro Patrício.
This paper discusses the use of the Shepard Tone (ST) as a digital sound source in musical composition. This tone has two musical interests. First, it underlines the difference between the tone height and the tone chroma, opening new possibilities in sound generation and musical perception. And second, considering the fact that it is (in a paradoxical way) locally directional while still globally stable and circumscribed it allows us to look differently at the instrument's range as well as at the phrasing in musical composition. Thus, this paper proposes a method of generating the ST relying upon an alternative spectral envelope, which as far as we know, has never been used before for the reproduction of the Shepard Scale Illusion (SSI). Using the proposed digital sound source, it was possible to successfully reproduce the SSI, even when applied to a melody. The melody was called "Perpetual Melody Auditory Illusion" because when it is heard it creates the auditory illusion that it never ends, as is the case with the SSI. Moreover, we composed a digital music titled "Perpetual Melody – contrasting moments", using exclusively the digital sound source as sound generator and the melody as musical content.

11.20h: [OS1-2] AN IN-SITU STUDY OF REAL LIFE LISTENING CONTEXT.
Diane Watson and Regan L. Mandryk.
Current models of musical mood are based on clean, noiseless data that does not correspond to real life listening experiences. We conducted an experience sampling study collecting in-situ data of listening experiences. We show that real life music listening experiences are far from the homogeneous experiences used in current models of musical mood.

11.40h: [OS1-3] EFFECTS OF AUDIO-TACTILE FLOOR AUGMENTATION ON PER-CEPTION AND ACTION DURING WALKING: PRELIMINARY RESULTS.
Stefano Papetti and Federico Fontana.
Two pilot experiments have been conducted to investigate the influence of auditory and underfoot tactile cues respectively on perception and action during walking. The for- mer experiment shows that illusory tactile perception can be generated, biased by the intensity of

auditory cues in the low-frequency region. The latter experiment suggests that non-visual foot-level augmentation may influence the gait cycle in normally able subjects. In the respective limits of significance, taken together both experiments suggest that the introduction of ecological elements of augmented reality at floor level may be exploited for the development of novel multimodal interfaces.

12.00h: [OS1-4] FACTORS IN HUMAN RECOGNITION OF TIMBRE LEXICONS GENERATED BY DATA CLUSTERING.
Gerard Roma, Anna Xambó, Perfecto Herrera, and Robin Laney.
Since the development of sound recording technologies, the palette of sound timbres available for music creation was extended way beyond traditional musical instruments. The organization and categorization of timbre has been a common endeavor. The availability of large databases of sound clips provides an opportunity for obtaining data-driven timbre categorizations via content-based clustering.

Oral Session 2: MODELING AND UNDERSTANDING
14.30h – 16.10h, Thursday, July 12th, 2012
Chair: *Georgios Marentakis*

14.30h: [OS2-1] SIMULATED FORMANT MODELING OF ACCOMPANIED SINGING SIGNALS FOR VOCAL MELODY EXTRACTION.
Yu-Ren Chien, Hsin-Min Wang, and Shyh-Kang Jeng.
This paper deals with the task of extracting vocal melodies from accompanied singing recordings. The challenging aspect of this task consists in the tendency for instrumental sounds to interfere with the extraction of the desired vocal melodies, especially when the singing voice is not necessarily predominant among other sound sources. Existing methods in the literature are either rule-based or statistical. It is difficult for rule-based methods to adequately take advantage of human voice characteristics, whereas statistical approaches typically require large-scale data collection and labeling efforts. In this work, the extraction is based on a model of the input signals that integrates acoustic-phonetic knowledge and real-world data under a probabilistic framework. The resulting vocal pitch estimator is simple, determined by a small set of parameters and a small set of data. Tested on a publicly available dataset, the proposed method achieves a transcription accuracy of 76%.

14.50h: [OS2-2] PHYSICAL MODELING AND HYBRID SYNTHESIS FOR THE GYIL AFRICAN XYLOPHONE.
Daniel Godlovitch, Tiago F. Tavares, Shawn Trail, and George Tzanetakis.
In this paper we introduce a physical model of the Gyil, an African pentatonic idiophone whose wooden bars' sonic characteristics most closely resemble the western marimba. We are most interested in the resonators of the instrument, which are comprised of graduated gourds suspended beneath each bar similar to the way tuned tubes are used on western

mallet instruments. The prominant characteristic of the resonator that we are concerned with is the intentionally added buzz that results when the bar is struck creating a naturally occuring type of distortion. Sympathetic distortion is inherent to African sound design, as these unamplified acoustic instruments must typically be heard above large crowds of people dancing and singing at ceremonies and festivals. The Gyil's distortion is a result of a specific preparation of the gourds where holes are drilled into the sides and covered with a membrane traditionally constructed from the silk of spider egg casings stretched across the opening. In analysing the sonic characteristics of the Gyil, and developing a model, we find that the physical mechanisms through which the characteristic Gyil sound is produced are highly non-linear, and the development of this model has required the use of synthesis techniques novel to physical modelling. We present several variants of our physical model, and conduct comparitive listening tests with musicians who are recognised Gyil virtuosos.

15.10h: [OS2-3] INVERSE PROBLEM IN SOUND SYNTHESIS AND MUSICAL CRE-ATION USING MASS-INTERACTION NETWORKS.
Jerome Villeneuve and Claude Cadoz.
Sound synthesis with mass-interaction physical modeling networks can be considered as a general paradigm capable of being the central part of complete software environments for musical creation. GENESIS 3, built around the CORDIS-ANIMA formalism and developed by ACROE/ICA Laboratory, is the first environment of this kind. Using it, the artist may be facing an inherent problematic of every creation process: how to use a given tool in order to obtain an expected result. In our context, the question would be: "Considering a sound, which physical model could produce it?". This paper especially aims at presenting the frame in which this inverse problem is set and at establishing its very own "ins and outs". However, we will also present two different algorithmic resolutions applied on quite simple cases and then discuss their relevance.

15.30h: [OS2-4] EXPLORING SOUND AND SPATIALIZATION DESIGN ON SPEAKER ARRAYS USING PHYSICAL MODELLING.
Georgios Marentakis and David Pirro.
In the course of the realization of the sound installation *Interstices*, questions pertaining to the auditory perception of location and extent and the spatial composition of the micro and macro structure of sound were explored in a *poietic* way. Physical modelling was re-interpreted as a framework to design the spatial and timbral appearance of sounds upon a set of distributed speaker array clusters. This explorative process lead to observations that helped formulating novel research questions within the context of psychoacoustics and auditory display.

15.50h: [OS2-5] SAXOPHONE BY MODEL AND MEASUREMENT.
Tamara Smyth and Srikanth Cherla.
This work presents an extension to a measurement technique that was used to estimate the reflection and transmission functions of musical instrument bells, to be used within the context of a parametric waveguide model. In the original technique, several measurements are

taken of a system, a 2-meter long cylindrical tube with a speaker and co-located microphone at one end, having incrementally varying termination/boundary conditions. Each measured impulse response yields a sequence of multiple evenly spaced arrivals, from which estimates of waveguide element transfer functions, including the bell reflection and transmission, may be formed. The use of the technique for measuring the saxophone presents difficulties due to 1) the inability of separating the bore from the bell for an isolated measurement, 2) the length of the saxophone producing impulse response arrivals that overlap in time (and are not easily windowed), and 3) the presence of a junction when appending the saxophone to the measurement tube and the spectral "artifact" generated as a result. In this work we present a different post signal processing technique to overcome these difficulties while keeping the hardware the same. The result is a measurement of the saxophone's round-trip reflection function which is used to construct its transfer function—the inverse transform of which yield's the instrument's impulse response.

Oral Session 3: SONIC INTERACTIONS
16.30h – 18.10h, Thursday, July 12th, 2012
Chair: *Davide Rocchesso*

16.30h: [OS3-1] "MUSICA SULL'ACQUA": A MOTION TRACKING BASED SONIFI-CATION OF AN AQUARIUM IN REAL TIME.
Stefano Baldan, Luca Andrea Ludovico, and Davide Andrea Mauro.
This paper presents a temporary multimedia installation set up at the *Civic Aquarium of Milan*. Thanks to four web cameras located in front of the tropical fishpond, fishes are tracked and their movements are used to control a number of music-related parameters in real time. In order to process multiple video streams, the open-source programming language Processing has been employed. Then, the sonification is implemented by a PureData patch. The communication among the parts of the system has been realized through Open Sound Control (OSC) messages.

16.50h: [OS3-2] ELECTRONIC PIPE ORGAN USING AUDIO FEEDBACK.
Seunghun Kim and Woon Seung Yeo.
This paper presents a new electronic pipe organ based on positive audio feedback. Unlike typical resonance of a tube of air, we use audio feedback introduced by an amplifier, a lowpass filter, as well as a loudspeaker and a microphone in a closed pipe to generate resonant sounds without any physical air blows. Timbre of this sound can be manipulated by controlling the parameters of the filter and the amplifier. We introduce the design concept of this audio feedback-based wind instrument, and present a prototype that can be played by a MIDI keyboard.

17.10h: [OS3-3] USE OF SOUNDSCAPES FOR PROVIDING INFORMATION ABOUT DISTANCE LEFT IN TRAIN JOURNEYS.
Kjetil Falkenberg Hansen and Roberto Bresin.
The study at hand presents the testing of sonification for communicating the distance between two stations in a train journey. We wanted to investigate if it is possible to provide the traveller with information about the distance left to the next station by using non-speech sounds. The idea is that of using a sonification that is independent from culture and language and that can be understood by international travellers.

17.30h: [OS3-4] EMPLOYING SPATIAL SONIFICATION OF TARGET MOTION IN TRACKING EXERCISES.
Simone Spagnol, Michele Geronazzo, Federico Avanzini, Fabio Oscari, and Giulio Rosati and.
This paper presents the results of an experiment in which the effect of spatial sonification of a moving target on the user's performance during the execution of basic tracking exercises was investigated. Our starting hypothesis is that a properly designed multimodal continuous feedback could be used to represent temporal and spatial information that can in turn improve performance and motor learning of simple target following tasks. Sixteen subjects were asked to track the horizontal movement of a circular visual target by controlling an input device with their hand. Two different continuous task-related auditory feedback modalities were considered, both simulating the sound of a rolling ball, the only difference between them being the presence or absence of binaural spatialization of the target's position. Results demonstrate how spatial auditory feedback significantly decreases the average tracking error with respect to visual feedback alone, contrarily to monophonic feedback. It was thus found how spatial information provided through sound in addition to visual feedback helps subjects improving their performance.

17.50h: [OS3-5] THE FIREFADER AND DERIVATIVES: SIMPLE, OPEN-SOURCE, AND RECONFIGURABLE HAPTICS FOR MUSICIANS.
Edgar Berdahl and Alexandros Kontogeorgakopoulos.
The FireFader is a simple haptic force-feedback device that is optimized for introducing musician to haptics. It has a single degree of freedom and is based upon a mass-produced linear potentiometer fader coupled to a DC motor, also known as a "motorized fader." Lights are connected in parallel with the motor to help visually communicate the strength of the force. Compatibile with OS X, Linux, and Windows, the FireFader consists of only open-source hardware and software elements. Consequently, it is also relatively easy for users to repurpose it into new projects involving varying kinds and numbers of motors and sensors. An open-source device driver for the FireFader allows it to be linked to a laptop via USB, so that the computer can perform the feedback control calculations. For example, the laptop can simulate the acoustics of a virtual musical instrument to calculate the motor force as a function of the fader position. The serial interface over USB causes delay of the control signal, but it facilitates easy programming and less expensive control nevertheless using floating-point computation. Some new devices derived from the FireFader design are presented.

Oral Session 4: HUMANITIES AND CULTURE
11.00h – 12.40h, Friday, July 13th, 2012
Chair: *Mark Grimshaw*

11.00h: [OS4-1] CREATIVE AGENTS, CURATORIAL AGENTS, AND HUMAN-AGENT INTERACTION IN COMING TOGETHER.
Arne Eigenfeldt and Philippe Pasquier.
We describe a multi-agent systems which composes in real-time, using negotiation as the active compositional technique. In one version of the system, creative agents' output is written to disk; during performance, a curatorial agent selects prior-composed movements and assembles a complete musical composition. The resulting score is then displayed to musicians, and performed live. A second version of the system is described, in which the real-time interaction is performed immediately by a mechanical musical instrument, and a human instrumentalist's performance data is included in system as being one of the agents (a human agent).

11.20h: [OS4-2] NOVICE COLLABORATION IN SOLO AND ACCOMPANIMENT IMPROVISATION.
Anne-Marie Hansen and Hans Jørgen Andersen.
This study investigates how non-musicians engaged in a solo-accompaniment music improvisation relationship. Seven user teams interacted with two electronic music instruments integrated in two pen tablets. One instrument was a melody instrument and the other a chord instrument. The study was done in order to understand how future shared electronic music instruments can be designed to encourage non-musicians to engage in social action through music improvisation. A combination of quantitative and qualitative analysis was used to find characteristics in co-expression found in a solo-accompaniment relationship. Results of interaction data and video analysis show that 1) teams related to each other through their experience with verbal conversation, 2) users searched for harmonic connections and 3) were able to establish rhythmical grounding. The paper concludes with some design guidelines for future solo-accompaniment shared improvisation interfaces: How realtime analysis of co-expression can be mapped to additional sound feedback that supports, strengthens and evolves co-expression in improvisation.

11.40h: [OS4-3] THE BODY IN ELECTRONIC MUSIC PERFORMANCE.
Jan C. Schacher.
This text discusses the notions of physical presence, perception and 'gestural' actions as an important element of a performance practice in electronic music. After discussing the meaning of the term 'gesture' in music and dance, a brief overview about current trends and methods in research is presented. The skills associated with the performance of electronic instruments are compared to those acquired with traditional instruments, for other physical performing arts such as dance and in technologically mediated art forms that extend the concept of the stage. Challenges and approaches for composing and performing electronic music are ad-

dressed and finally a tentative statement is made about embodiment as a quality and category to be applied to and perceived in electronic music performance.

12.00h: [OS4-4] DESIGNING SIMULACRA OR THE ELECTRONIC REPLICATION OF A MECHANICAL INSTRUMENT.
Fabio Kaiser, Marian Weger, and Winfried Ritsch.
Specific requirements of certain works of music, especially in the field of contemporary experimental music of the 19th century, are sometimes hard to meet when it comes to the performance. Special instruments or technologies are necessary and often no longer available, broken or their documentation is insufficient. This paper addresses this problem of performance practice in contemporary music by exploring the design of an electronic replacement of a mechanical instrument for the performance of the piece "Mouvement - vor der Erstarrung" by Helmut Lachenmann. The simulacra developed consist of a musical interface, a software for sound synthesis and a loudspeaker system. A focus is put on the challenge of synthesising and projecting the sound as close as possible to the original instrument and to fit the musical requirements of the piece. The acoustic integration of the electronic instrument into an ensemble of acoustic instruments was achieved by using an omni-directional loudspeaker. For the sound synthesis, a hybrid approach of sampling and additive synthesis was chosen. The prototypes developed were proven to be robust and reliable and the simulacra were generally well-accepted by performing musicians, surrounding musicians, conductor and audience.

12.20h: [OS4-5] VIRTUAL MASKS IN THE BACCHAE BY GEORGIA SPIROPOULOS (IRCAM,2010) : EXPLORING TRAGIC VOCALITY IN MAX/MSP ENVIRONMENT.
Georgia Spiropoulos, Anastasia Georgaki, and Petras Giorgos.
In this paper we present some technical aspects on the interactive masks created by the composer Georgia Spiropoulos for the needs of the opera Les Bacchantes (Ircam, 2010). Bacchae is an opera for a single performer, tape and live electronics where the voice of the performer interprets four different roles with the interactive environment in Max/MSP. The virtual masks as a metaphor of Euripides' dramatic personae in which masks of the same actor are used as virtual scores which register the vocal trace of the performer and give further vocal agility, extensibility, mutation, multiplication and augmented vocality.

Oral Session 5: INTERFACES
14.30h – 15.50h, Friday, July 13th, 2012
Chair: *Dan Overholt*

14.30h: [OS5-1] PAPERTONNETZ: MUSIC COMPOSITION WITH INTERACTIVE PAPER.
Louis Bigo, Jérémie Garcia, Antoine Spicher, and Wendy Mackay.
Tonnetz are space-based musical representations that lay out individual pitches in a regular structure. They are primarily used for analysis with visualization tools or on paper and

for performance with button-based tablet or tangible interfaces. This paper first investigates how properties of Tonnetz can be applied in the composition process, including how to represent pitch based on chords or scales and lay them out in a two-dimensional space. We then describe PaperTonnetz, a tool that lets musicians explore and compose music with Tonnetz representations by making gestures on interactive paper. Unlike screen-based interactive Tonnetz systems that treat the notes as playable buttons, PaperTonnetz allows composers to interact with gestures, creating replayable patterns that represent pitch sequences and/or chords. We describe the results of an initial test of the system in a public setting, and how we revised PaperTonnetz to better support three activities: discovering, improvising and assembling musical sequences in a Tonnetz. We conclude with a discussion of directions for future research with respect to creating novel paper-based interactive music representations to support musical composition.

14.50h: [OS5-2] SURFACE AS STRUCTURE: THE MULTI-TOUCH CONTROLLER AS MAP OF MUSICAL STATE SPACE.

Oliver Bown, Daniel Jones, and Sam Britton.
In this paper we present a new general approach to the use of multi-touch screens as musical controllers. In our approach the surface acts as a large hierarchically structured state-space map through which a musician can navigate a path. We discuss our motivations for this approach, which include the possibility of representing large amounts of musical data such as an entire live set in a common visually mnemonic space rather like a map, and the potential for a rich dynamic and non-symbolic approach to live algorithm generation. We describe our initial implementation of the system and present some initial examples of its use in musical contexts.

15.10h: [OS5-3] A HIERARCHICAL APPROACH FOR THE DESIGN OF GESTURE-TO-SOUND MAPPINGS.

Jules Françoise, Baptiste Caramiaux, and Frédéric Bevilacqua.
We propose a hierarchical approach for the design of gesture-to-sound mappings, with the goal to take into account multilevel time structures in both gesture and sound processes. This allows for the integration of temporal mapping strategies, complementing mapping systems based on instantaneous relationships between gesture and sound synthesis parameters. Specifically, we propose the implementation of Hierarchical Hidden Markov Models to model gesture input, with a flexible structure that can be authored by the user. Moreover, some parameters can be adjusted through a learning phase. We show some examples of gesture segmentations based on this approach, considering several phases such as preparation, attack, sustain, release. Finally we describe an application, developed in Max/MSP, illustrating the use of accelerometer-based sensors to control phase vocoder synthesis techniques based on this approach.

15.30h: [OS5-4] SPATIAL RENDERING OF AUDIO-TACTILE FEEDBACK FOR EX-PLORATION AND OBJECT INTERACTION IN VIRTUAL ENVIRONMENTS.
Roberto Pugliese, Archontis Politis, and Tapio Takala.
In this paper an integrated system for the creation of a combined audio and tactile display is described. In order to get an illusion of physically being among virtual sounding objects, we used vibration motors attached to a belt to give tactile stimulus, and sensed the user's position and orientation with a 3D tracker. Collisions with free-to-move virtual objects is provided through semi-realistic vibration on the correct collision point with respect to the position and orientation of the user. The tactile vibration is encoded on 8 vibrotactile motors using a calculation of the gains on the motors similar to a panning law and improved to convey the perceptual illusion of proximity of the object and collision with it. We combine the tactile stimulus with a spatialization system augmented with distance cues.

Oral Session 6: MUSIC INFORMATION RETRIEVAL
11.00h – 12.40h, Saturday, July 14th, 2012
Chair: *Bob Sturm*

11.00h: [OS6-1] BUILDING A MUSIC SEARCH DATABASE USING HUMAN COM-PUTATION.
Mark Cartwright and Bryan Pardo.
Systems able to find a song based on a sung, hummed, or whistled melody are called Query-By-Humming (QBH) systems. Hummed or sung queries are not directly compared to origi-nal recordings. Instead, systems employ search keys that are more similar to a cappella singing than the original pieces. Successful, deployed systems use human computation to create search keys: hand-entered midi melodies or recordings of a cappella singing. There are a number of human computation-based approaches that may be used to build a database of QBH search keys, but it is not clear what the best choice is based on cost, computation time, and search performance. In this paper we compare search keys built through human computation using two populations: paid local singers and Amazon Mechanical Turk workers. We evaluate them on quality, cost, computation time, and search performance.

11.20h: [OS6-2] TOWARDS PREDICTING EXPRESSED EMOTION IN MUSIC FROM PAIRWISE COMPARISONS.
Jens Madsen, Bjørn Sand Jensen, Jan Larsen, and Jens Brehm Nielsen.
We introduce five regression models for the modeling of expressed emotion in music using data obtained in a two alternative forced choice listening experiment. The predictive perfor-mance of the proposed models is compared using learning curves, showing that all models converge to produce a similar classification error. The predictive ranking of the models is compared using Kendall's tau rank correlation coefficient which shows a difference despite similar classification error. The variation in predictions across subjects and the difference in

ranking is investigated visually in the arousal-valence space and quantified using Kendall's tau.

11.40h: [OS6-3] COMBINING SCORE AND FILTER BASED MODELS TO PREDICT TEMPO FLUCTUATIONS IN EXPRESSIVE MUSIC PERFORMANCES.
Florian Krebs and Maarten Grachten.
Tempo variations in classical music are an important means of artistic expression. Fluctuations in tempo can be large and sudden, making applications like automated score following a challenging task. Some of the fluctuations may be predicted from (tempo annotations in) the score, but prediction based only on the score is unlikely to capture the internal coherence of a performance. On the other hand, filtering approaches to tempo prediction (like the Kalman filter) are suited to track gradual changes in tempo, but do not anticipate sudden changes.

12.00h: [OS6-4] MODELING AND PREDICTING SONG ADJACENCIES IN COMMERCIAL ALBUMS.
Andy M. Sarroff and Michael Casey.
This paper examines whether latent structure may be discovered from commercially sold albums using features characterizing their songs adjacencies. We build a large-scale dataset from the first 5 songs of 8,505 commercial albums. The dataset spans multiple artists, genres, and decades. We generate a training set (Train) consisting of 11,340 True song adjacencies and use it to train a mixture of multivariate gaussians. We also generate two disjoint test sets (Test1 and Test2), each having 11,340 True song adjacencies and 45,360 Artificial song adjacencies. We perform feature subset selection and evaluate on Test_1. We test our model on Test_2 in a standard retrieval setting. The model achieves a precision of 22.58%, above baseline precision of 20% . We compare this performance against a model trained and tested on a smaller dataset and against a model that uses full-song features. In the former case, precision is better than the large scale experiment (24.80%). In the latter case, the model achieves precision no better than baseline (20.13%). Noting the difficulty of the retrieval task, we speculate that using features which characterize song adjacency may improve Automatic Playlist Generation (APG) systems.

12.20h: [OS6-5] AUDIO METAPHOR: AUDIO INFORMATION RETRIEVAL IN[A]MOMENT.
Miles Thorogood, Philippe Pasquier, and Arne Eigenfeldt.
We have developed an audio information retrieval system called, Audio Metaphor, that utilizes large online collaborative databases for real time soundscape composition. Audio Metaphor has been used in a contemporary dance piece IN[A]MOMENT. The audience interacts with the system by sending the system Tweets. At the heart of the Audio Metaphor is a sub-query generation algorithm. This algorithm which we name SLiCE, for string list chopping experiments, accepts a natural language phrase that is parsed into a text feature string list, which is chopped into sub-query search to find a combination of queries with non-empty

mutually exclusive results. Employing SLiCE, Audio Metaphor processes natural language phrases to find a combination of audio file results that represents the input phrase. In parallel, the parsed input phrase is used to search for related Tweets which are similarly put through SLiCE. Search results are then sent to a human composer to combine and process into a soundscape.

Oral Session 7: SYNTHESIS
14.30h – 16.10h, Saturday, July 14th, 2012
Chair: *Tamara Smyth*

14.30h: [OS7-1] EVEN MORE ERRANT SOUND SYNTHESIS.
Nick Collins.
Sound synthesis algorithms which radically depart from acoustical equations, and seek out numerical quirks at audio rate, can still have a part to play in the art-science investigations of computer music. This paper describes a host of ideas in alternative sound synthesis, from dilation equations and nonlinear dynamical equations, through probabilistic sieves, to oscillators based on geometrical formulae. We close with some new ideas in concatenative sound synthesis, using sparse approximation as the analysis method for matching, and driving synthesis through an EEG interface.

14.50h: [OS7-2] AUTOMATIC CALIBRATION OF MODIFIED FM SYNTHESIS TO HARMONIC SOUNDS USING GENETIC ALGORITHMS.
Matthieu Macret, Philippe Pasquier, and Tamara Smyth.
Many audio synthesis techniques have been successful in reproducing the sounds of musical instruments. Several of these techniques require parameters calibration. However, this task can be difficult and time-consuming especially when there is not intuitive correspondence between a parameter value and the change in the produced sound. Searching the parameter space for a given synthesis technique is, therefore, a task more naturally suited to an automatic optimization scheme.

15.10h: [OS7-3] LCSYNTH: A STRONGLY-TIMED SYNTHESIS LANGUAGE THAT INTEGRATES OBJECTS AND MANIPULATIONS FOR MICROSOUNDS.
Hiroki Nishino and Naotoshi Osaka.
In this paper, we describe LCSynth, a new sound synthe-sis language currently under development. LCSynth integrates objects and manipulation for microsounds in its language design. Such an integration of objects and manipulations for microsound into sound synthe-sis framework design can facilitate creative exploration in the mi-crosound synthesis techniques such as granular synthesis and waveset synthesis, which has been considered relatively

difficult in the existing sound synthesis frameworks and computer music languages, which depend solely on traditional abstraction of unit-generators.

15.30h: [OS7-4] CONCATENATIVE SYNTHESIS UNIT NAVIGATION AND DYNAMIC REARRANGEMENT IN VRGRAINS.
Victor Zappi, Dario Mazzanti, Andrea Brogni, and Darwin Caldwell.
Corpus based concatenative synthesis has been approached from different perspectives by many researchers. This generated a number of diverse solutions addressing the matter of target selection, corpus visualization and navigation. With this paper we introduce the concept of extended descriptor space, which permits the arbitrary redistribution of audio units in space, without affecting each unit's sonic content. This feature can be exploited in novel instruments and music applications to achieve spatial dispositions which could enhance control and expression. Making use of Virtual Reality technology, we developed vrGrains, an immersive installation in which real-time corpus navigation is based on the concept of extended descriptor space and on the related audio unit rearrangement capabilities. The user is free to explore a corpus represented by 3D units which physically surrounds her/him. Through natural interaction, the interface provides different interaction modalities which allow controllable and chaotic audio unit triggering and motion.

15.50h: [OS7-5] SKETCHING CONCATENATIVE SYNTHESIS: SEARCHING FOR AUDIOVISUAL ISOMORPHISM IN REDUCED MODES.
Augoustinos Tsiros, Gregory Leplatre, and Michael Smyth.
This paper presents a prototype allowing the control of a concatenative synthesis algorithm using a 2D sketching interface. The design of the system is underpinned by a preliminary discussion in which isomorphisms between auditory and visual phenomena are identified. We support that certain qualities of sound and graphics are inherently cross-modal. Following this reasoning, a mapping strategy between low-level auditory and visual features was developed. The mapping enables the selection of audio units based on five feature data streams that derive from the statistical analysis of the sketch.

Oral Session 8: PROCESSING SOUND AND MUSIC
16.30h – 18.10h, Saturday, July 14th, 2012
Chair: *Gianpaolo Evangelista*

16.30h: [OS8-1] THE CONSTANT-Q IIR FILTERBANK APPROACH TO SPECTRAL FLUX.
Risto Holopainen.
Spectral flux is usually measured with the FFT, but here a constant-Q IIR filterbank implementation is proposed. This leads to a relatively efficient sliding feature extractor with the benefit of keeping the time resolution of the output as high as it is in the input signal. Several applications are considered, such as estimation of sensory dissonance, uses in sound

synthesis, adaptive effects processing and visualisation in recurrence plots. A novel feature called second order flux is also introduced.

16.50h: [OS8-2] PERSISTENT EMPIRICAL WIENER ESTIMATION WITH ADAPTIVE THRESHOLD SELECTION FOR AUDIO DENOISING.
Kai Siedenburg.
Exploiting the persistence properties of signals leads to significant improvements in audio denoising. This contribution derives a novel denoising operator based on neighborhood smoothed, Wiener filter like shrinkage. Relations to the sparse denoising approach via thresholding are drawn. Further, a rationale for adapting the threshold level to a performance criterion is developed. Using a simple but efficient estimator of the noise level, the introduced operators with adaptive thresholds are demonstrated to act as attractive alternatives to the state of the art in audio denoising.

17.10h: [OS8-3] ENHANCED SOURCE-FILTER MODEL OF QUASI-HARMONIC INSTRUMENTS FOR SOUND SYNTHESIS, TRANSFORMATION AND INTERPOLATION.
Henrik Hahn and Axel Roebel.
In this paper we present a new instrument model to be used for sound modification and interpolation. The approach comprises the analysis of sounds of an instruments sound database, a parameter estimation for the instrument model and a sound synthesis using this model. The sound analysis is carried out by the segmentation of each sound into a sinusoidal and noise component. Both components are modeled using B-splines (basic-splines) in a n-dimensional hyperplane according to the specific sound parameters to capture the instruments timbre for its complete pitch range, possible intensities and temporal evolution. Sound synthesis therein is achieved by exploring these hyperplanes and altering the timbre of the sounds of the database. To conclude a subjective evaluation is presented for comparison with state of the art sound transformations. This work is based on a preliminary study published recently.

17.30h: [OS8-4] PHASE VOCODERS WITH ARBITRARY FREQUENCY BAND SELECTION.
Gianpaolo Evangelista, Monika Dörfler, and Ewa Matusiak.
Time-frequency representations play a central role in sound analysis and synthesis. While the most conventional methods are based on phase vocoders with uniform frequency bands, perception and physical characteristics of sound signals suggest the need for nonuniform bands. In this paper we propose a flexible design of a phase vocoder having arbitrary frequency band divisions. The design is based on recently developed nonuniform frames where here frequency warping, i.e. a remapping of the frequency axis, is employed for the design of the sliding windows, which are different for each frequency channel. We show that tight frames can be obtained with this method, which allow for perfect reconstruction with identical anal-

ysis and synthesis time-frequency atoms. The transform and its inverse have computationally efficient implementations.

17.50h: [OS8-5] AUTOMATIC ARRANGEMENT FOR GUITARS USING HIDDEN MARKOV MODEL.

Gen Hori, Yuma Yoshinaga, Satoru Fukayama, Hirokazu Kameoka, and Shigeki Sagayama.

Considering a large population of guitarist and a relatively poor selection of guitar scores, there should be a certain demand for systems that automatically arrange scores for other instruments to guitar scores. This paper introduces a framework based on hidden Markov model (HMM) that carries out "arrangement" and "fingering determination" in a unified way. The framework takes forms and picking patterns as its hidden states and a given piece of music as an observation sequence and carries out fingering determination and arrangement as a decoding problem of HMM. With manually-set HMM parameters reflecting preference of beginner guitarists, the framework generates natural fingerings and arrangements suitable for beginners. Some examples of fingering and arrangement generated by the framework are presented.

Poster Craze presentations take place in the Auditorium.
Poster Sessions take place in the main entrance and lobby.

Poster Craze 1: SYNTHESIS OF MUSIC AND AUDIO
10.00h – 10.15h, Thursday, July 12th, 2012
Chair: *Nick Collins*

Poster Session 1
13.00h – 14.30h, Thursday, July 12th, 2012

[PS1-1] YIG, THE FATHER OF SERPENTS: A REAL-TIME NETWORK MUSIC PERFORMANCE ENVIRONMENT.
Chad McKinney and Nick Collins.
Approaches to network music performance are often focused on creating systems with minimal latency and maximal synchronicity. In this article we present *Yig, the Father of Serpents*, a new program for performing network music that is designed with these principles in mind, but also offers an argument for a different approach. In Yig, users may have identical states yet the audio rendering could be different. In this paper an introduction to the interface is followed by a brief description of the technical development of the software. Next, the instrument is classified and analyzed using existing frameworks and some philosophy behind divergence in network music is explained. The article concludes with an numeration of potential software improvements and suggestions towards future work using divergence

[PS1-2] AN AUTOMATED TESTING SUITE FOR COMPUTER MUSIC ENVIRON-MENTS.
Nils Peters, Trond Lossius, and Timothy Place.
Software development benefits from systematic testing with respect to implementation, optimization, and maintenance. Automated testing makes it easy to execute a large number of tests efficiently on a regular basis, leading to faster development and more reliable software. Systematic testing is not widely adopted within the computer music community, where software patches tend to be continuously modified and optimized during a project. Consequently, bugs are often discovered during rehearsal or performance, resulting in literal "show stoppers". This paper presents a testing environment for computer music systems, first developed

for the Jamoma framework and Max. The testing environment works with Max 5 and 6, is independ from any 3rd-party objects, and can be used with non-Jamoma patches as well.

[PS1-3] ON THE PERFORMANCE OF REAL-TIME DSP ON ANDROID DEVICES. *André J. Bianchi and Marcelo Queiroz.*
With the spread of mobile devices comes the possibility of using (relatively) cheap, wireless hardware embedded with plenty of sensors to perform real time Digital Signal Processing on live artistic performances. The Android Operating System represents a milestone for mobile devices due to its lightweight Java Virtual Machine and API that makes it easier to develop applications that run on any (supported) device. With an appropriate DSP model implementation, it is possible to use the values of sensors as input for algorithms that can modify streams of audio to generate rich output signals. Because of memory, CPU and battery limitations, it is interesting to study the performance of each device under real time DSP conditions, and also provide feedback about resources consumption to provide the basis for (user or automated) decision making regarding devices' use. This work presents an object oriented model for performing DSP on Android devices and focus on measuring the time taken to perform common DSP tasks as read from the input, write to output, and carry the desired signal manipulation. We obtain statistics regarding one specific combination of device model and operating system version, but our approach can be used on any Android device to provide the user with important information that can aid aesthetic and algorithmic decisions.

[PS1-4] A REACTIVE, CONFLUENTLY PERSISTENT FRAMEWORK FOR THE DESIGN OF COMPUTER MUSIC SYSTEMS.
Hanns Holger Rutz.
The process of composition can be seen as sequence of manipulations on the material. In algorithmic composition, such sequences are prescribed through another set of sequences which yield the algorithm. In a realtime situation the sequences may be closely linked to the temporal sequence of the unfolding musical structure, but in general they form orthogonal temporal graphs on their own. We present a framework which can be used to model these temporal graphs. The framework is composed of layers, which—from low to high level—provide (1) database storage and software transactional memory with selectable temporal semantics, (2) the most prominent semantics being confluent persistence, in which the temporal traces are registered and can be combined, yielding a sort of structural feedback or recursion, and finally (3) an event and expression propagation system, which, when combined with confluent persistence, provides a hook to update dependent object graphs even when they were constructed in the future. This paper presents the implementation of this framework, and outlines how it can be combined with a realtime sound synthesis system.

[PS1-5] STRINGSCORE: COMPOSING MUSIC WITH VISUAL TEXT.
Jesus L. Alvaro.
This paper introduces StringScore, a productive text-based Music Representation for Composition that provides a visual arrangement of motivic elements in a compact and meaningful layout of characters. Time dimension is represented horizontally, taking the text character as the time unit, thus considering character strings as time-lines where musical elements are sequenced. While being compact, Stringscore provides a high degree of independent control of the fundamentals of traditional composition, such as musical form, harmony, melodic contour, texture and counterpoint. The description of the proposed representation has been illustrated with musical examples of applied composition. As an additional validation, StringScore has been successfully applied in the analysis and re-composition of the beginning of Beethoven's Fifth Symphony. Finally, the paper presents "StringScore in the Cloud", a Web-based implementation that probes the representation in the environment of the Computer Music Cloud.

[PS1-6] THE FLUXATIONS STOCHASTIC INTERACTIVE ALGORITHMIC MUSIC ENGINE (SIAME) AND IPHONE APP.
Joshua Mailman.
This paper reports on aspects of the Fluxations paradigm for interactive music generation and an iPhone app implementation of it. The paradigm combines expressive interactivity with stochastic algorithmic computer generated sound. The emphasis is on pitch-oriented (harmonic) continuity and flux, as steered through sliders and sensors. The paradigm enables the user-performer to maximize exotic but audible musical variety by spontaneously manipulating parameters within the paradigm.

[PS1-7] WAVEGUIDES IN SONIFICATION.
Katharina Vogt, Robert Höldrich, and David Pirrò.
Digital waveguides have been used in signal processing for modelling room acoustics. The same technique can be used for model-based sonifications, where the given data serves to construct the three-dimensional sound propagation model. The resulting sounds are intuitive to understand as they simulate real world acoustics. As an example we introduce a digital waveguide mesh based on complex data of computational physics. This approach allows exploring sonically this three-dimensional data and unveiling spatial structures.

[PS1-8] AUTOMATIC MELODIC GRAMMAR GENERATION FOR POLYPHONY MUSIC USING A CLASSIFIER SYSTEM.
Tsubasa Tanaka and Kiyoshi Furukawa.
In this paper, we propose a method to generate new melodic styles (melodics) in the automatic composition of polyphonic music. In the proposed method, a melodic style is represented as a grammar that consists of rewriting rules, and the rewriting rules are generated by a classifier system, which is a genetics-based machine learning system. In the previous studies of the grammatical approach, the problem of how to treat polyphony and that of generating

new melodic styles automatically haven't been studied very intensively. Therefore, we have chosen to tackle those problems. We modeled the generative process of polyphonic music as asynchronous growth by applying rewriting rules in each voice separately. In addition, we developed a method to automatically generate grammar rules, which are the parameters of the polyphony model. The experimental results show that the proposed method can generate grammar rules and polyphonic music pieces that have characteristic melodic styles.

[PS1-9] COMPUTATIONALLY CREATIVE IMPROVISATION.
Benjamin Smith and Guy Garnett.
Models of computational creativity promise to provide insight into the nature of human creative work and innovation. Intrinsically motivated, automated, creative agents present a potential avenue for the exploration of creativity in the arts, and in music in particular. A novel reinforcement learning agent designed to improvise music in a self-motivated fashion is described, formulated to prove the capabilities of an artificially creative musical system. The prototype employs unsupervised adaptive resonance theory algorithms to model theories of human perception, cognition, and creativity. While the generated results are constrained for initial evaluation further extensions suggest the potential to create meaningful, aesthetically valuable compositions.

[PS1-10] THE QUIET WALK: SONIC MEMORIES AND MOBILE CARTOGRAPHY.
Alessandro Altavilla and Atau Tanaka.
This paper presents The Quiet Walk, an interactive mo-bile artwork for sonic explorations of urban space. The goal of TQW is to find the "quietest place". An interface on the mobile device directs the user to avoid noisy areas of the city, giving directions to find quiet zones. Data collected by the system generates a geo-acoustic map of the city that facilitates the personal recollection of sonic memories. The system is comprised of 3 components: a smartphone running a custom application based on libpd and openFrameworks, a web server collecting the GPS and acoustical data, and computer in an exhibition space displaying a visualization of the sound map. This open-ended platform opens up possibilities of mobile digital signal processing, not only for sound art related artworks but also as a platform for data-soundscape compositions and mobile, digital explorations in acoustic ecology studies.

[PS1-11] STATISTICAL SYNTHESIS OF TRANSIENT AND PITCH-CHANGING SIGNALS.
Sofia Cavaco.
We propose a statistical method for modeling and synthesizing sounds with both sinusoidal and attack transient components. In addition, the sinusoidal component can have pitch-changing characteristics. The method applies multivariate decomposition techniques (such as independent component analysis and principal component analysis) to learn the intrinsic structures that characterize the sound samples. Afterwards these structures are used to synthesize new sounds which can be drawn from the distribution of the real original sound

samples. Here we apply the method to impact sounds and show that the method is able to generate new samples that have the characteristic attack transient of impact sounds.

[PS1-12] COMPOSING GRAPHIC SCORES AND SONIFYING VISUAL MUSIC WITH THE SUM TOOL.

Sara Adhitya and Mika Kuuskankare.

This paper will explore the potential for the SUM tool, intended initially for the sonification of images, as a tool for graphical computer-aided composition. As a user li- brary with a graphical user interface within the computer- aided composition environment of PWGL, SUM has the potential to be used as a graphical approach towards com- puter-aided composition. Through the re-composition of the graphic score of Ligeti's Artikulation, we demonstrate how SUM can be used in the generation of a graphic score. Supporting spatio-temporal timepaths, we explore alterna- tive ways of reading this score. Furthermore, we investi- gate the claim of certain visual artworks to be 'visual mu- sic', by sonifying them as graphic scores in SUM.

Poster Craze 2: INTERACTIONS
10.00h – 10.15h, Friday, July 13th, 2012
Chair: *Olga Timcenko*

Poster Session 2
13.00h – 14.30h, Friday, July 13th, 2012

[PS2-1] A SYSTEM FOR SKETCHING IN HARDWARE: DO-IT-YOURSELF INTER-
FACES FOR SOUND AND MUSIC COMPUTING.
Daniel Overholt.
A system for Do-It-Yourself (DIY) interface designs focused on sound and music computing
has been developed. The system is based on the Create USB Interface (CUI), which is an
open source microcontroller prototyping board together with the GROVE system of interchangeable transducers. Together, these provide a malleable and fluid prototyping process of
'Sketching in Hardware' for both music and non-music interaction design ideas. The most
recent version of the board is the CUI32Stem, which is designed specifically to work hand-in-
hand with the GROVE elements produced by Seeed Studio, Inc. GROVE includes a growing
collection of open source sensors and actuators that utilize simple 4-wire cables to connect
to the CUI32Stem. The CUI32Stem itself utilizes a high-performance Microchip® PIC32
microcontroller, allowing a wide range of programmable interactions. The development of
this system and its use in sound and music interaction design is described. Typical use scenarios for the system may pair the CUI32Stem with a smartphone, a normal computer, and
one or more GROVE elements via wired or wireless connections.

[PS2-2] A STUDY OF THE NOISE-LEVEL IN TWO INFRARED MARKER-BASED
MOTION CAPTURE SYSTEMS.
Alexander Refsum Jensenius, Kristian Nymoen, Ståle A. Skogstad, and Arve Voldsund.
With musical applications in mind, this paper reports on the level of noise observed in two
commercial infrared marker-based motion capture systems: one high-end (Qualisys) and one
affordable (OptiTrack). We have tested how various features (calibration volume, marker size,
sampling frequency, etc.) influence the noise level of markers lying still, and fixed to subjects
standing still. The conclusion is that the motion observed in humans standing still is usually
considerably higher than the noise level of the systems. Dependent on the system and its
calibration, however, the signal-to-noise-ratio may in some cases

[PS2-3] SENSOR SETUP FOR FORCE AND FINGER POSITION AND TILT MEA-
SUREMENTS FOR PIANISTS.
Tobias Großhauser, Victor Candia, and Bernd Tessendorf.
Finger force, acceleration and position are fundamental in playing music instruments. Mea-
suring these parameters is a technical challenge and precise position and acceleration mea-
surement of single fingers is particularly demanding. We present a sensor setup for multi

modal measurements of force, position and acceleration in piano playing. We capture outputs from the upper extremity contributing to the total force output seen at the fingers. To precisely characterize fingers' positions and acceleration we use wearable sensors. A 6-axes (3-force and 3-torque axes) force sensor precisely captures contributions from hand, wrist and arm. A finger's acceleration sensor and a MIDI grand piano complete the measuring setup. The acceleration and position sensor is fixed to the dorsal aspect of the last finger phalanx. The 6-axes sensor is adjustable to fit individual hand positions and constitutes a basis setup that can be easily expanded to account for diverse measurement needs. An existing software tool was adapted to visualize the sensor data and to synchronize it to the MIDI out. With this basis setup we seek to estimate the isolated force output of finger effectors and to show coherences of finger position, force and attack. To proof the setup, a few pilot measurements were carried out.

[PS2-4] DISEMBODIED VOICES: A KINECT VIRTUAL CHOIR CONDUCTOR.
Marcella Mandanici and Sylviane Sapir.
"Disembodied voices" is an interactive environment designed for an expressive, gesture-based musical performance. The motion sensor Kinect, placed in front of the performer, provides the computer with the 3D space coordinates of the two hands. The application is designed according to the metaphor of the choir director: the performer, through gestures, is able to run a score and to produce a real-time expressive interpretation. The software, developed by the authors, interprets the gestural data by activating a series of compositional algorithms that produce vocal sounds. These are pre-recorded samples processed in real time through the expressive interaction dependent on the conductor's gestures. Hence the name of the application: you follow the conductor's gestures, hear the voices but don't see any singer. The system also provides a display of motion data, a visualization of the part of the score performed at that time, and a representation of the musical result of the compositional algorithms activated.

[PS2-5] A HYBRID KEYBOARD-GUITAR INTERFACE USING CAPACITIVE TOUCH SENSING AND PHYSICAL MODELING.
Christian Heinrichs and Andrew McPherson.
This paper presents a hybrid interface based on a touch-sensing keyboard which gives detailed expressive control over a physically-modeled guitar. Physical modeling allows realistic guitar synthesis incorporating many expressive dimensions commonly employed by guitarists, including pluck strength and location, plectrum type, hand damping and string bending. Often, when a physical model is used in performance, most control dimensions go unused when the interface fails to provide a way to intuitively control them. Techniques as foundational as strumming lack a natural analog on the MIDI keyboard, and few digital controllers provide the independent control of pitch, volume and timbre that even novice guitarists achieve. Our interface combines gestural aspects of keyboard and guitar playing. Most dimensions of guitar technique are controllable polyphonically, some of them continuously within each

note. Mappings are evaluated in a user study of keyboardists and guitarists, and the results demonstrate its playability by performers of both instruments.

[PS2-6] A FRAMEWORK TO EVALUATE THE ADOPTION POTENTIAL OF INTERACTIVE PERFORMANCE SYSTEMS FOR POPULAR MUSIC.
Nicolas Gold.
Popular music plays a central role in the lives of millions of people. It motivates beginners, engages experienced musicians, and plays both functional (e.g. churches) and non-functional (e.g. music festivals) roles in many contexts. Forming and maintaining a popular music ensemble can be challenging, particularly for part-time musicians who face other demands on their time. Where an ensemble has a functional role, performing music of consistent style and quality becomes imperative yet the demands of everyday life mean that it is not always possible to have a full complement of musicians. Interactive music technology has the potential to substitute for absent musicians to give a consistent musical output. However, the technology to achieve this (for popular music) is not yet mature, or in a suitable form for adoption and use by musicians who are not experienced with interactive music systems, or who are unprepared to work in experimental music or with experimental systems (a particular concern for functional ensembles).

[PS2-7] A MULTI-TIMELINES SCHEDULER AND A REHEARSAL FUNCTION FOR IMPROVING USERS' SENSATION OF ORCHESTRAL CONDUCTING WITH A CONDUCTING SYSTEM.
Takashi Baba, Mitsuyo Hashida, and Haruhiro Katayose.
The VirtualPhilharmony (VP) system conveys the sensation of conducting an orchestra to a user (a conductor). VP's performances are created through interaction between the conductor and orchestra, exactly like real performance. "Concertmaster function" has been already implemented by incorporating the heuristics of conducting an orchestra. A precisely predictive scheduler and dynamical template have been designed based on analyses of actual recordings. We especially focused on two more problems to emulate a more real orchestral performance; one was that each note in the template was controlled by single-timeline scheduler; the other was that the interaction and communication between the conductor and the orchestra in repeated practices were not simulated. We implemented "Multi-timelines scheduler" and "Rehearsal function" to resolve these problems.

[PS2-8] AN EXTENSION OF INTERACTIVE SCORES FOR MULTIMEDIA SCENARIOS WITH TEMPORAL RELATIONS FOR MICRO AND MACRO CONTROLS.
Mauricio Toro-Bermudez, Myriam Desainte-Catherine, and Julien Castet.
Software to design multimedia scenarios is usually based either on a fixed timeline or on cue lists, but both models are unrelated temporally. On the contrary, the formalism of interactive scores can describe multimedia scenarios with flexible and fixed temporal relations among the objects of the scenario, but cannot express neither temporal relations for micro controls nor signal processing. We extend interactive scores with such relations and with sound process-

ing. We show some applications and we describe how they can be implemented in Pure Data. Our implementation has low average relative jitter even under high CPU load.

[PS2-9] PIANIST MOTION CAPTURE WITH THE KINECT DEPTH CAMERA.
Aristotelis Hadjakos.

Capturing pianist movements can be used for various applications such as music performance research, musician medicine, movement-augmented piano instruments, and piano pedagogical feedback systems. This paper contributes an unobtrusive method to capture pianist movements based on depth sensing. The method was realized using the Kinect depth camera and evaluated in comparison with 2D marker tracking.

[PS2-10] CREATIVE EXPERIMENTS USING A SYSTEM FOR LEARNING HIGH-LEVEL PERFORMANCE STRUCTURE IN ABLETON LIVE.
Aengus Martin, Craig Jin, Benjamin Carey, and Oliver Bown.

The Agent Design Toolkit is a software suite that we have developed for designing the behaviour of musical agents; software elements that automate some aspect of musical composition or performance. It is intended to be accessible to musicians who have no expertise in computer programming or algorithms. However, the machine learning algorithms that we use require the musician to engage with technical aspects of the agent design, and our research goal is to find ways to enable this process through understandable and intuitive concepts and interfaces, at the same time as developing effective agent algorithms.

[PS2-11] GESTURAL MUSICAL AFFORDANCES.
Atau Tanaka, Alessandro Altavilla, and Neal Spowage.

This paper is a comparative study of gestural interaction with musical sound, designed to gain insight into the notion of musical affordance on interactive music systems. We conducted an interview base user study trialing three accelerometer based devices, an iPhone, a Wii-mote, and an Axivity Wax prototype, with four kinds of musical sound, including percussion, stringed instruments, and voice recordings. The accelerometers from the devices were mapped to computer based sound synthesis parameters. By using consistent mappings across different source sounds, and performing them from the three different devices, users experienced forms of physical, sonic, and cultural affordance, that combine to form what we term musical affordance.

[PS2-12] PATHS IN INTERACTIVE SOUND VISUALIZATION: FROM AVOL TO AV CLASH.
Nuno N. Correia.

This paper compares two multimodal net art projects, AVOL and AV Clash, by the author and André Carrilho (under the name Video Jack). Their objective is to create projects enabling integrated audiovisual expression that are flexible, intuitive, playful to use and engaging to experience. The projects are contextualized with related works. The methodology for the research is presented, with an emphasis on experience-focused Human-Computer Interaction (HCI) perspectives. The comparative evaluation of the projects focuses on the analysis of the answers to an online questionnaire. AVOL and AV Clash have adopted an Interactive Audiovisual Objects (IAVO) approach, which is a major contribution from these projects, consisting of the integration of sound, audio visualization and Graphical User Interfaces (GUI). Strengths and weaknesses detected in the projects are analysed. Generic conclusions are discussed, mainly regarding simplicity and harmony versus complexity and serendipity in audiovisual projects. Finally, paths for future development are presented.

[PS2-13] REMOTE MUSIC TUITION.

Sam Duffy, Doug Williams, Ian Kegel, Tim Stevens, Jack Jansen, Pablo Cesar, and Patrick Healey.

It is common to learn to play an orchestral musical instrument through one-to-one lessons with an experienced tutor. For musicians who choose to study performance at an undergraduate level and beyond, their tutor is an important part of their professional musical development. For many musicians, travel is part of their professional lives due to touring, auditioning and teaching, often overseas. This makes temporary separation of students from their tutor inevitable. A solution used by some conservatoires is teaching via video conferencing, however the challenges of using video conference for interaction and collaborative work are well documented. The Remote Music Tuition prototype was designed to enhance music tuition via video conference by providing multiple views of the student. This paper describes the system, documents observations from initial tests of the prototype and makes recommendations for future developments and further testing.

Poster Craze 3: MUSIC INFORMATICS
10.00h – 10.15h, Saturday, July 14th, 2012
Chair: *Sofia Dahl*

Poster Session 3
13.00h – 14.30h, Saturday, July 14th, 2012

[PS3-1] AUTOMATIC AND MANUAL ANNOTATION OF TIME-VARYING PERCEPTUAL PROPERTIES IN MOVIE SOUNDTRACKS.
Vedant Dhandhania, Jakob Abesser, Anna Marie Kruspe, and Holger Grossman.
In this paper, we present an automated process as a part of the SyncGlobal project for time continuous prediction of loudness and brightness in soundtracks. The novel Annotation Tool is presented, which allows performing manual time-continuous annotations. We rate well-known audio features to represent two perceptual attributes -loudness and brightness. A regression model is trained with the manual annotations and the acoustic features representing the perceptions. Four different regression methods are implemented and their success in tracking the two perceptions is studied. A coefficient of determination (R2) of 0.91 is achieved for loudness and 0.35 for brightness using Support Vector Regression (SVR), yielding a better performance than Friberg et al. (2011).

[PS3-2] EVALUATING HOW DIFFERENT VIDEO FEATURES INFLUENCE THE VISUAL QUALITY OF RESULTANT MOTIONGRAMS.
Alexander Refsum Jensenius.
Motiongrams are visual representations of human motion, generated from regular video recordings. This paper evaluates how different video features may influence the generated motiongram: inversion, colour, filtering, background, lighting, clothing, video size and compression. It is argued that the proposed motiongram implementation is capable of visualising the main motion features even with quite drastic changes in all of the above mentioned variables.

[PS3-3] CONTENT-BASED RETRIEVAL OF ENVIRONMENTAL SOUNDS BY MULTIRESOLUTION ANALYSIS.
Ianis Lallemand, Diemo Schwarz, and Thierry Artières.
Query by example retrieval of environmental sound recordings is a research area with applications to sound design, music composition and automatic suggestion of metadata for the labeling of sound databases. Retrieval problems are usually composed of successive feature extraction (FE) and similarity measurement (SM) steps, in which a set of extracted features encoding important properties of the sound recordings are used to compute the distance between elements in the database. Previous research has pointed out that successful features in the domains of speech and music, like MFCCs, might fail at describing environmental sounds, which have intrinsic variability and noisy characteristics. We present a set of novel

multiresolution features obtained by modeling the distribution of wavelet subband coefficients with generalized Gaussian densities (GGDs). We define the similarity measure in terms of the Kullback-Leibler divergence between GGDs. Experimental results on a database of 1020 environmental sound recordings show that our approach always outperforms a method based on traditional MFCC features and Euclidean distance, improving retrieval rates from 51% to 62%.

[PS3-4] CHORD RECOGNITION USING PREWITT FILTER AND SELF-SIMILARITY. *Nikolay Glazyrin and Alexander Klepinin.*
In this paper we propose a method of audio chord estimation. It does not rely on any machine learning technique, but shows good recognition quality compared to other known algorithms. We calculate a beat-synchronized spectrogram with high time and frequency resolution. It is then processed with an analogue of Prewitt filter used for edge detection in image processing to suppress non-harmonic spectral components. The sequence of chroma vectors obtained from spectrogram is smoothed using self-similarity matrix before the actual chord recognition. Chord templates used for recognition are binary-like, but have the tonic and the 5th note accented. The method is evaluated on the 13 Beatles albums.

[PS3-5] CONSTRUCTING HIGH-LEVEL PERCEPTUAL AUDIO DESCRIPTORS FOR TEXTURAL SOUNDS. *Thomas Grill.*
This paper describes the construction of computable audio descriptors capable of modeling relevant high-level perceptual qualities of textural sounds. These qualities - all metaphoric bipolar and continuous constructs - have been identified in previous research: high-low, ordered-chaotic, smooth-coarse, tonal-noisy, and homogeneous-heterogeneous, covering timbral, temporal and structural properties of sound.

[PS3-6] RECOGNITION OF PHONEMES IN A-CAPPELLA RECORDINGS USING TEMPORAL PATTERNS AND MEL FREQUENCY CEPSTRAL COEFFICIENTS. *Jens Kofod Hansen.*
In this paper, a new method for recognizing phonemes in singing is proposed. Recognizing phonemes in singing is a task that has not yet matured to a standardized method, in comparison to regular speech recognition. The standard methods for regular speech recognition have already been evaluated on vocal records, but their performances are lower compared to regular speech. In this paper, two alternative classification methods dealing with this issue are proposed. One uses Mel-Frequency Cepstral Coefficient features, while another uses Temporal Patterns. They are combined to create a new type of classifier which produces a better performance than the two separate classifiers. The classifications are done with US English songs. The preliminary result is a phoneme recall rate of 48.01% in average of all audio frames within a song.

[PS3-7] SPATDIF: PRINCIPLES, SPECIFICATION, AND EXAMPLES.
Nils Peters, Trond Lossius, and Jan C. Schacher.
SpatDIF, the Spatial Sound Description Interchange Format, is an ongoing collaborative effort offering a semantic and syntactic specification for storing and transmitting spatial audio scene descriptions. The SpatDIF core is a lightweight minimal solution providing the most essential set of descriptors for spatial sound scenes. Additional descriptors are introduced as extensions, expanding the namespace and scope with respect to authoring, scene description, rendering and reproduction of spatial audio. A general overview of the specification is provided, and two use cases are discussed, exemplifying SpatDIF's potential for file-based pieces as well as real-time streaming of spatial audio scenes.

[PS3-8] NEW FRAMEWORK FOR SCORE SEGMENTATION AND ANALYSIS IN OPENMUSIC.
Jean Bresson and Carlos Pérez-Sancho.
We present new tools for the segmentation and analysis of musical scores in the OpenMusic computer-aided composition environment. A modular object-oriented framework enables the creation of segmentations on score objects and the implementation of automatic or semi-automatic analysis processes. The analyses can be performed and displayed thanks to customizable classes and callbacks. Concrete examples are given, in particular with the implementation of a semi-automatic harmonic analysis system and a framework for rhythmic transcription.

[PS3-9] IDEAS IN AUTOMATIC EVALUATION METHODS FOR MELODIES IN ALGORITHMIC COMPOSITION.
Alan Freitas, Frederico Gadelha Guimaraes, and Rogerio Barbosa.
Algorithmic Composition (AC) methods often depend on evaluation methods in order to define the probabilities that change operators have to be applied. However, the evaluation of music material involves the codification of aesthetic features, which is a very complex process if we want to outline automatic procedures that are able to compute the suitability of melodies. In this context, we offer in this paper a comprehensive investigation on numerous ideas to examine and evaluate melodies, some of them based on music theory. These ideas have been used in music analysis but have been usually neglected in many AC procedures. Those features are partitioned into ten categories. While there is still much research to do in this field, we intend to help computer-aided composers define more sophisticated and useful methods for evaluating music.

[PS3-10] MUSICOG: A COGNITIVE ARCHITECTURE FOR MUSIC LEARNING AND GENERATION.
James B. Maxwell, Arne Eigenfeldt, Philippe Pasquier, and Nicolas Gonzalez Thomas.
Music composition is an intellectually demanding human activity that engages a wide range of cognitive faculties. Although several domain-general integrated cognitive architectures (ICAs) exist—ACT-R, Soar, Icarus, etc.—the use of integrated models for solving musical

problems remains virtually unexplored. In designing MusiCOG, we wanted to bring forward ideas from our previous work, combine these with principles from the fields of music perception and cognition and ICA design, and bring these elements together in an initial attempt at an integrated model. Here we provide an introduction to MusiCOG, outline the operation of its various modules, and share some initial musical results.

[PS3-11] ENUMERATION OF CHORD SEQUENCES.
Nick Collins.

The enumeration of musical objects has received heightened attention in the last twenty five years, and whilst such phenomena as tone rows, polyphonic mosaics, and scales have been explored, there has not been prior investigation of the enumeration of chord sequences. In part, analysts may have disregarded the situation as having a trivial solution, namely the number of chord types at each step raised to the power of the number of steps. However, there are more subtle and interesting situations where there are constraints, such as rotational and transpositional equivalence of sequences. Enumeration of such chord sequences is explored through the application of Burnside's lemma for counting equivalence classes under a group action, and computer generation of lists of representative chord sequences outlined. Potential extensions to 'McCartney's Chord Sequence Problem' for the enumeration of cyclic (looping) chord sequences are further discussed

[PS3-12] THE ICST DSP LIBRARY: A VERSATILE AND EFFICIENT TOOLSET FOR AUDIO PROCESSING AND ANALYSIS APPLICATIONS.
Stefano Papetti.

The ICST DSP library is a compact collection of C++ routines with focus on rapid development of audio processing and analysis applications. Unlike other similar libraries it offers a set of technical computing tools as well as speed-optimized industrial-grade DSP algorithms, which allow one to prototype, test and develop real-time applications without the need of switching development environment. The package has no dependence on third-party libraries, supports multiple platforms and is released under FreeBSD license.

[PS3-13] AN OVERVIEW OF SOUND AND MUSIC APPLICATIONS FOR ANDROID AVAILABLE ON THE MARKET.
Gaël Dubus, Kjetil Falkenberg Hansen, and Roberto Bresin.

This paper introduces a database of sound-based applications running on the Android mobile platform. The long-term objective is to provide a state-of-the-art of mobile applications dealing with sound and music interaction. After exposing the method used to build up and maintain the database using a non-hierarchical structure based on tags, we present a classification according to various categories of applications, and we conduct a preliminary analysis of the repartition of these categories reflecting the current state of the database.

Music Program

Wednesday, July 11ᵀᴴ, 2012

20.00 – Concert: Electro-acoustic Music
Den Frie Centre of Contemporary Art
Oslo Plads 1
Dk - 2100 Copenhagen Ø
http://denfrie.dk/

Curator: *Spencer Topel*

Program

Pierre Alexandre Tremblay: *La Rupture Inéluctable* for bass clarinet and electronics (Heather Roche, bass clarinet)

Akira Takaoka: *Responsorium* , for voice and electronics (Signe Asmussen, Figura Ensemble)

Judith Shatin: *Cherry Blossom and a Wrapped Thing; After Hokusai* for clarinet and electronics (Anna Klett, Figura Ensemble)

Jesper Holmen: *XP* for saw, clarinet, double bass and electronics (Figura Ensemble) Invited Danish composer.

Panayiotis Kokoras: *T-totum* for amplified snare drum and electronics (Frans Hansen, Figura Ensemble)

—INTERMISSION—

Spencer Topel: *Svin* for double bass and electronics (Jesper Egelund, Figura Ensemble)

Alex Harker: *Fluence* for clarinet and electronics (Heather Roche, clarinet)

João Pedro Oliveira: *Vox Sum Vitae* for percussion and electronics (Frans Hansen, Figura Ensemble)

Judith Shatin: *Grito del Corazón* for ensemble and electronics (Figura Ensemble)

1. Pierre Alexandre Tremblay: *La Rupture Inéluctable* (Four meditations on our metastable states. For Heather) for bass clarinet and electronics.
Heather Roche, bass clarinet

I. Vanitas vanitatum omnia vanitas
(Vanity of vanities; all is vanity)

Ecclesiastes

II. Memento Mori
(Remember you will die)

Latin phrase

III. Timor mortis conturbat me
(the fear of death disturbs me)

third Nocturn of Matins of the Office of the Dead

IV. Carpe diem quam minimum credula postero
(Seize the Day, trusting as little as possible in the future)

Horace, Odes

Happiness is so fragile, a kind of precarious and improbable balance: a multicolour soap bubble. How can one fully enjoy it despite the vertigo its transience induces? It seems that reflection on impermanence was, and forever will be, at the heart of self-conscience, both for the individual and society. This permanence should soothe me.
© Pierre Alexandre Tremblay, 2011

2. Akira Takaoka: *Responsorium* for voice and electronics (Signe Asmussen, Figura Ensemble)

I have always marveled at the mastery of Renaissance composers. *Responsorium* is my first attempt, modeled after Missa pro defunctis (1605) by late Renaissance Spanish composer Tomas Luis de Victoria, to build a rule system that makes possible the integration of plainchant melodies into twelve-tone harmonies.

The piece consists of "Cantus" sections and contrasting "Versus" ones. While harmonies are rather static in the Cantus sections, pitch-class sets are constantly transformed in the Versus sections according to the pitches of the D-Dorian melody. As a result, the twelve-tone harmonies give an illusion that they sound as if they were intrinsic components of the modal melody.

All the voice leading and the transformations are strictly regulated by the rule system implemented in my own Java program. The program generated score files for the sound synthesis and processing software RTcmix, which processes the vocal sounds and produces all the synthesized sounds.

3. Judith Shatin: *Cherry Blossom and a Wrapped Thing; After Hokusai* for clarinet and electronics (Anna Klett, Figura Ensemble))

Cherry Blossom and a Wrapped Thing; After Hokusai (2004, rev 2006) was inspired by a print of the same name made by the extraordinary Japanese printmaker known as Hokusai (1760 - 1849). I encountered it in a sumptuous collection of his prints at the Otani Museum in Tokyo and was immediately struck by the subtle mystery of both its subject matter and execution. The cherry blossom speaks of the beauty and brevity of life; the wrapped thing of its ineffability. My composition, commissioned by clarinetist F. Gerard Errante for his CD Delicate Balance, is scored for amplified clarinet and 8- channel or stereo audio. The electronics sometimes wrap around the performer and audience, sometimes drift to earth, at others float, while the clarinet delicately responds to them. All processing was designed with RTcmix. –JS

4. Jesper Holmen: *XP* for saw, clarinet, double bass and electronics (Figura Ensemble)

XP was written for a Christmas concert in 2003. The title's two letters are part of the Greek christ monogram chi-rho (an referring to feast) and the standard abbreviation of the words "express paye" as you write on mail to be brought out quickly (referring to that the work was commissioned nine days before the concert), part of the two middle letters in my name (referring to that I wrote the piece).

The original version of *XP* was for clarinet. Since then I have made a variety of versions for other instruments. At this concert first performance by Figura with a new version for saw, clarinet, double bass and electronics.

5. Panayiotis Kokoras: *T-totum* for percussion and electronics (Frans Hansen, Figura Ensemble)

T-totum is a sound composition on the motion of rotation. The recordings of the electronic part comes from objects rotating on top and around the snare drum like various types of spinning tops, a cappuccino plate, glass-balls, motor shaker and other. The percussionist interacts with electronic part using various drivers to excite the snaredrum. The piece requires from the musician to develop virtuosity on sound rather than on complex rhythms.

The title comes from a type of top, usually having four lettered sides, that is used to play various games of chance.

T-totum make use of sonic rhetoric such as 'associations' in a way that abstract sounds recall known every day listening sounds like airplane, helicopter, steps, wind, seashore etc. These two worlds build a story within story creating association of ideas and as result degrees of ambiguity.

An interactive version of the piece was finalist at the 2nd European competition for live-electronic music projects 2009 at Goteborg / Sweden. www.panayiotiskokoras.com.

6. Spencer Topel: *Svin* for double bass and electronics (Jesper Egelund, Figura Ensemble)

A sound I rarely heard while visiting Europe throughout my life comes from the Harley Davidson motorcycle. This gas-guzzling mainstay in American towns—a symbol of the working-class—is largely despised by liberal Americans and sometimes associated with biker gangs such as the Hell's Angels. Yet, from a sonic perspective, the Harley is a unique sound icon, yielding a rich, semi-chaotic, baritone timbre. As a child growing up in Colorado, I recall swarms of leather-clad bikers riding through the Rocky Mountains on their adorned "Hogs," a term sometimes used to describe the Harley.

It was years later, when I heard Gérard Grisey's Partiels (1975) for the first time, with the brash contrabass solo at the beginning that the sensation of hearing these large motorcycles came back to me, and it is the collision of these two experiences that contextualizes the materials in this piece. SVIN in turn explores the potential of the contrabass as means of generating the "energy" required to activate the harmonics from Partiels, and to explore the timbal similarities with a recording of a journey through middle-America on a Harley motorcycle.

7. Alex Harker: *Fluence* for clarinet and electronics (Heather Roche, clarinet)

In several recent pieces I have explored the idea of the co-existence of two musical worlds. In one time and pitch are articulated clearly and cleanly, as if on a grid, in the other things are blurred, unclear and constantly morphing. *Fluence* takes this idea and places the two worlds side-by-side, although the temporal grid in this case is treated as if it were elastic, constantly stretched and compressed.

In *Fluence* I was able to, for the first time, devise a system in which I could create a kind of 'real-time tape' music, constructing the electronic part from samples in a way that remains flexible in performance. Each gesture in the electronic part is constructed from a bank of over a thousand clarinet samples. Samples are almost never specified directly, rather the computer selects samples using audio descriptor matching, according to certain shapes and parameters. Thus, each time the electronic part is realised is slightly different. *Fluence* was commissioned by Ergodos (ergodos.ie) with funds from the Irish Arts Council.

8. João Pedro Oliveira: *Vox Sum Vitae* for percussion and electronics (Frans Hansen, Figura Ensemble)

"I am the voice of life" is an inscription in a church bell in Strasbourg. In one of my trips to perform an organ concert in Germany, on a Sunday morning I was woke suddenly with the sound of hundreds of church bells, announcing the early morning church service. This piece is a representation of that sound image.

9. Judith Shatin: *Grito del Corazón* for ensemble and electronics (Figura Ensemble)

Grito del Corazón was inspired by Goya's "Black Paintings. " When the Ensemble Barcelona Nuova Musica approached me to commission a piece for their Painting Music program, I immediately recalled my response to these paintings in the Prado, and suggested this theme. The paintings deal with terrifying subject matter, such as Saturn devouring his Son (Saturno Devorando a su Hijo). I met videographer Katherine Aoki at the MacDowell Artist Colony, and we decided to collaborate on this project. *Grito del Corazón* was premiered at the VIII Festival de Cinema Independent de Alternative 2001 in Barcelona, and has since been internationally presented at venues ranging from the Staedlejik Museum in Amsterdam, to the Festival Sonoimágenes in Buenos Aires the Ai-Maako Festival in Santiago, and New York's Knitting Factory. The music includes electronics and an instrumental score with guided improvisation, with parts available for a variety of solos and instrumental combinations. –JS

THURSDAY, JULY 12ᵀᴴ, 2012

20.00 – Concert: Music for Novel Instruments and Interfaces
Overgaden
Institut for Samtidskunst
Overgaden Neden Vandet 17
DK-1414 København K
http://www.overgaden.org/

Curator: *Chikashi Miyama*

Program

Atau Tanaka and Adam Parkinson: *Adam and Atau* for 4 hands iPhone

Yuta Uozumi and Keisuke Oyama: *Four Fragments* for swarming robotics

Dan Tramte: *Corse Mode* for straight key and electronics

Dimitri Paile and Johan Snell: *Brain Music* – musical output by thought

Butch Rovan and Lucky Leone: *Slim Jim Choker* for typewriter, voice and electronics

Chikashi Miyama: *Treble Motion* for Qgo

Atau Tanaka and Adam Parkinson
Adam and Atau **for 4 hands iPhone**
Adam & Atau exploit a commonly available consumer electronics device, a smartphone, as an expressive, gestural musical instrument. The device is well known an iconic object of desire in our society of consumption, playing music as a fixed commodity. The performers re-appropriate the mobile phone and transform the consumer object into an instrument for concert performance. As a duo, with one in each hand, they create a chamber music, 4-hands iPhone. The accelerometers allow high precision capture of the performer's free space gestures. This drives a granular synthesis patch in Pure Data (PD), where one patch becomes the process by which a range of sounds from the natural world are stretched, frozen, scattered, and restitched. The fact that all system components - sensor input, signal processing and sound synthesis, and audio output, are embodied in a single device make it a self-contained, expressive musical instrument.

Yuta Uozumi
Four Fragments **for swarming robotics**
This performance aims to approach the next style of "mashup" and/or "Cut-up" via fusion of paradigms of artificial-life and turntable. We developed a system named "SoniCell" to

realize it. SoniCell employs four robots called "cell". Each cell behaves as a metaphor of life based on a simple interaction model with prey-predator relationship. Each cell is assigned a music-track in the manner of turntable.

Therefore, the system reconstructs and mixes the music-tracks via cells' interactions and performers' interventions. In this framework, the aspects of the system and performers interactions and cells' internal-states create structures of sounds and music from different tracks.

Dan Tramte
Corse Mode: **for Straight Key and Electronics**

There are numerous similarities between morse code and text-messaging/internet lingo. Both are coded representations of [and are dependent upon] existing languages; both compress the textual message through acronyms and contractions of frequently used word/phrases; both resulted from the advent of a technological telecommunication advancement; both were products of constraints (small frequency bandwidth and low RF power as well as character limits); finally, both are modes for [nearly] instant communication across long distances.

The text (intentionally omitted from the program notes) is coded twice: First the word (for example 'Text') is translated into text-messaging/internet lingo (TXT), which is then translated into morse code (- -..- -).

Dimitri Paile
Brain Music – **musical output by thought**

Dimitri Paile's master's thesis from the Aalto University's School of Art and Design was a thought-controlled musical instrument. Dimitri proved that it is possible to consciously control and manipulate musical output by thought without tactile or gestural interaction. Instead of using prepared samples or existing virtual instruments, Dimitri works with the very fundaments of sound. The auditive output of his brain-instrument is based on basic audio synthesis methods, and ultimately creates a cerebrally triggered sound synthesis symphony. But you may begin to wonder; what implications does this have in relation to more atavistic musical expression?

Lucky Leone and Butch Rovan
Slim Jim Choker **for typewriter, voice and electronics**

A recital in ten parts for speaker & interactive typewriter

1. The Typing
2. The Endings
3. The Haiku
4. The Actions
5. The Story, part 1
6. The Nouns
7. The Reverse
8. The Story, part 2
9. The Consonants

10. The Poem

Slim Jim Choker is based on an absurd but true story about an unusual event that takes place one summer night. The content of the brief story is represented from a variety of perspectives in the ten movements, each of which reflects on the materiality of the telling.

The typewriter itself plays a role, producing in its sounds an alternative text that interrupts and counterpoints the speaking voice. The main interactive interface – an augmented vintage typewriter – controls real-time processing and synthesis.

Chikashi Miyama
Treble Motion for Qgo

In this performance, the performer wears Qgo, a pair of glove-shaped wireless wearable interface. The interface detects the movement of two hands and the distance between both hands, employing infrared sensors, accelerometers, and gyro sensors. Qgo digitizes the analog data from the sensors and transfers them to the host computer using Xbee Antenna. Based on the incoming data from Qgo, a software synthesizer running on the host computer generates electronic sounds. The synthesizer also analyzes the several aspects of the produced sound, such as amplitude, pitch, and spectral centroid, and forwards these data to a OpenGL-based realtime video processing software employing OSC messages. The video software processes the 3D image of the performer from a Kinect sensor in response to the incoming OSC messages. With this interactive system, this work attempts to realize the intimate and dynamic relationships amongst the human performer, the electronic sound, and the video image.

Friday, July 13th, 2012

16.00-19.00 – Sound Installation Walk
Begins at Medialogy, Aalborg University Copenhagen.
All installations are on display daily (2 to 7PM) from July 11 through July 14.

Curator: *Paula Matthusen*

Aalborg University Copenhagen
A.C. Meyers Vænge 15
DK-2450 Copenhagen

Martin Rumori: *inout*

Peter Batchelor: *Dome*

Damp Gallery
Esplanaden 1 C
1263 Copenhagen
http://dampgallery.dk/

Laura Maes: *Oorwonde*

Black Box Gallery
Fredericiagade 14 kld.
Ground Floor
1310 Copenhagen K
Denmark
http://www.blackboxgallery.dk/

Ted Apel: *Call and Resonance*

James Nesfield: *Canvas*

Paula Matthusen: *Work Divided by Time*

Martin Rumori: *inout*
The sound installation *inout* connects two auditory live situations through the mediation of technology. It is installed in an in-between place. Two pairs of microphones pick up two different, oppositely oriented sound situations. By means of a rotation tracked headphone, the listener may dive into either sound situation or a mixture of both by simply facing the corresponding direction.

inout declares both sound situations "auditive readymades" and mediates between them and the listener. As a consequence, it also leads the listener's attention to the act of listening itself.

inout is realised in embedded hardware. The digital tracking data is interpreted by a microcontroller which in turn controls four channels of zero-latency analogue attenuation circuitry.

Peter Batchelor: *DOME*

A series of transparent geodesic 'sound domes' are presented. Each dome houses 26 speakers which surround the listener who lies within. The speakers act together as a single coordinated sound-producing unit, presenting detailed spatialised sonic images over the surfaces of the domes. The perceived nature of each dome—its apparent material structure and its context—is determined by these sonic images. Listeners, shutting their eyes, may feel themselves to be contained within an enclosed structure, with rain pounding on the surface of what seems to be a corrugated iron 'roof', a roof that may then transform to become amorphous—composed of liquid that bubbles, trickles or gushes across the speaker-space before re-solidifying, receding, fragmenting and swirling around them. Or it may ultimately vanish altogether, presenting real-world sonic environments that are indistinguishable from the reality that exists beyond the dome.

Laura Maes: *Oorwonde*

The concept of *Oorwonde* is an aural surgery in which the visitor, aka the 'patient', hears and feels the soundtrack of a fictitious operation. The patient can influence various aspects of the sounds and determine the location where the sounds are reproduced.

The sounds are transmitted in various ways; four speakers, three electro-magnets, a vibrator motor and a piezoelectric disk are integrated into specific places in and on a stainless steel table. The person lying on the table can choose which sound producing sources to activate as an FSR is assigned to each sound source. Changing the pressure on an FSR has an immediate impact on the produced sound.

Oorwonde is as much a tactile experience as an auditory one as the sound waves emitted are designed to be felt. When standing next to the table the sounds produced can barely be heard.

Ted Apel: *Call and Resonance*

Five large tubes are used to impart strong resonances on hand made sound making circuits in each tube. Each circuit independently alternates between recording sound and playing back its recording. The sounds recorded are a combination of the sounds produced by the other tubes, the ambient sounds of the space and, the resonance of the tube. In this way, the combined soundfield is an emergent property of the five tubes, that is, each tubes sound is dependent on the contributions of the others.

James Nesfield: *Canvas*

Canvas explores our ideas of touch, perception and physicality through sound. The piece uses a virtual digital model of a metal plate which is mapped to the surface of a soft wood and canvas construction. In co-locating its digital and tangible components the *Canvas* allows its audience to interact, combine and explore the contrasting perceptual cues that contribute to our everyday understanding of physicality on both sides of the digital/physical divide.

Touching its surface in different ways, people can explore the nuances, combination and complex interplay of the physical behaviour from both the virtual model and the physical, tangible contraction of the canvas itself. Left untouched, the virtual physical model will produce a metallic shimmer from the movement of air across the material's surface.

This piece was developed as part of my Master's thesis at SARC, Queen's University Belfast under Dr Maarten van Walstijn and Prof. Sile O'Modhrain.

Paula Matthusen: *work divided by time*

work divided by time engages with the cultural concepts of power, energy, and time. The installation derives its inspiration in part from the intricate work of the Bily Brothers, who, working by candlelight and nestled within the Czech community of Spillville, Iowa, constructed mechanical clocks depicting the world reflected to them by newspaper and other printed publications at the beginning of the twentieth century. *work divided by time* creatively evokes the work of the Bily Brothers – clearly of a different era – to form a reflective space.

Special thanks to collaborator and technical assistant Néstor Prieto.
Thank you to the Astronomy Department of Wesleyan University, William Herbst, Linda Shettleworth. Many thanks to Kate Ten Eyck, Bruce Strickland, and David Strickland. Thank you to the CFA, in particular Pam Tatge, Barbara Ally, Erinn Roos-Brown, and Sewon Kang and the Music Department of Wesleyan, especially Ron Kuivila, Deborah Shore, and Sandra Brough. Thank you to Kate Klimesh and Carole Riehle of the Bily Clocks Museum for making the recordings of the clocks possible. Finally, thank you to Carl Matthusen, for assistance in recording and for the original introduction to work of the Bily Brothers.

work divided by time was commissioned by the Center for the Arts as a part of Feet to the Fire: Fueling the Future, made possible by grants from The Andrew W. Mellon Foundation and the Doris Duke Charitable Foundation, and with support from The Bily Clocks Museum in Spillville, Iowa.

SATURDAY, JULY 14TH, 2012

20.00 – Concert: Music Robots

Den Frie Centre of Contemporary Art
Oslo Plads 1
Dk - 2100 Copenhagen Ø
http://denfrie.dk/

Curators: *Expressive Machines Musical Instruments*

Program

Peter Van Zandt Lane: *Nebula Squeeze* for bassoon, AMI, and CARI (P. Van Zandt Lane, bassoon)

Arne Eigenfeldt: *Coming Together* EMMI for AMI, CARI and TAPI

Shawn Trail: ///// for extended Likembe and Gyil with AMI, CARI, and TAPI + DSP

Scott Miller: *Détente* for AMI, CARI, TAPI and Kyma

Nick Collins: *Blues for Nancarrow* for AMI, CARI and TAPI

Judith Shatin: *Sic Transit* for TAPI and percussion (Frans Hansen, percussion; Figura Ensemble)

Steven Kemper: *Microbursts* for AMI, CARI and TAPI

Troy Rogers: *Phantom Variations* for AMI, CARI and TAPI

Scott Barton: *From Here to There* for AMI, CARI and TAPI

Program Notes: See tonight's concert printouts.

BIOGRAPHIES

Curators

Spencer Topel's music has appeared on concert programs in venues such as Issue Project Room, Brooklyn NY, Orchestra Hall, Minnesota, the Chiesa di Sana Caterina Treviso in Venice, Italy, the Aspen Music Festival, Chigiana Festival in Siena, Italy, at Alice Tully and Weill Concert Halls in New York, and in Tokyo City Opera Hall. Mr. Topel has won awards and commissions from organizations such as Juilliard, Accademia Musicale Chigiana, American Modern Ensemble, ASCAP, BMI, Cornell University and from the National Foundation from Advancement in the Arts. This summer Mr. Topel starts as an Assistant Professor at Dartmouth College. Current projects include the curation of a st concert at Sound and Music Computing 2012 in Copenhagen, Denmark, and a CD project with GPR Records featuring newly composed songs for baritone and piano.

Chikashi Miyama is a composer, video artist, interface designer, and performer. He received a MA from Kunitachi College of Music, Tokyo, Japan, a Nachdiplom from Music academy of Basel, Switzerland, and a Ph.D from University at Buffalo, New York, USA. In 2011, he received a research grant from DAAD and worked as a visiting researcher at ZKM, Karlsruhe, Germany. His compositions have received an ICMA student award, a Chancellor's award from State University of New York, a second prize in SEAMUS commission competition, a special prize in Destellos Competition, and a honorable mention in the Residence Prize section of the Bourges Electroacoustic Music Competition. His works and papers have been accepted by ICMC twelve times, by NIME four times, and selected by various international festivals in more than 18 countries. He is currently teaching computer music as a lecturer at the college of music and dance in Cologne, Germany.

Paula Matthusen writes both electroacoustic and acoustic music and realizes sound installations. Her music has been performed by Alarm Will Sound, International Contemporary Ensemble (ICE), orchest de ereprijs, Dither Electric Guitar Quartet, Glass Farm Ensemble, Sideband, Orchestra of the League of Composers, Kathryn Woodard, James Moore, Jody Redhage, Todd Reynolds, Kathleen Supové, and Margaret Lancaster. Awards include a Fulbright Grant, two ASCAP Morton Gould Young Composers' Award, First Prize in the Young Composers' Meeting Composition Competition, the MacCracken and Langley Ryan Fellowship, a Van Lier Fellowship, and the Walter Hinrichsen Award from the American Academy of Arts and Letters. Matthusen is currently Assistant Professor of Music at Wesleyan University.

Expressive Machines Musical Instruments (EMMI) is a band of sonic thrill seekers, composers who have turned to the creation of novel robotic musical instruments to achieve their musical vision. Founded in Charlottesville by Troy Rogers, Scott Barton, and Steven Kemper in 2007, the group and their mechanical string, wind, and percussion instruments have turned heads and opened ears at festivals and venues throughout North America and Europe. Exploring the expanded palette of sounds offered by these new devices, the group provides audiences with a sonic and visual experience unlike any other.

Composers

GUEST COMPOSER

Judith Shatin is a composer and sound artist whose musical practice reflects her fascinations with literature and visual arts, with the sounding world, and with the social and communicative power of music. Called "something magical" by Fanfare, and "highly inventive on every level" by the Washington Post, her music has been honored with four awards from the National Endowment for the Arts and a two-year retrospective sponsored by the Lila Wallace Readers Digest Arts Partners Program. Commissions include those from the Barlow and Fromm Foundations, the McKim Fund of the Library of Congress, the Kronos Quartet, National Symphony, Scottish Voices and many more. Her music is widely performed and recorded, with her recent CD, Tower of the Eight Winds, on the Innova label. Judith Shatin is William R. Kenan, Jr. Professor of Music at the University of Virginia, where she founded and directs the Virginia Center for Computer Music. (www.judithshatin.com)

Concert 1

Pierre Alexandre Tremblay is a composer and a performer on bass guitar and sound processing devices, in solo and within the groups ars circa musicæ (Paris, France), de type inconnu (Montréal, Québec), and Splice (London, UK). His music is mainly released by Empreintes DIGITALes and Ora.

He is Reader in Composition and Improvisation at the University of Huddersfield (UK) where he also is Director of the Electronic Music Studios. He previously worked in popular music as producer and bassist, and is interested in videomusic and coding.

He likes oolong tea, reading, and walking. As a founding member of the no-tv collective, he does not own a working television set.

Akira Takaoka born in Tokyo, Japan, is a composer and music theorist. He is currently Professor of Music at Tamagawa University in Tokyo. He is also Lecturer and Research Associate at the Graduate School of Science and Engineering, Chuo University in Tokyo, where he directs research projects on music information retrieval and Visiting Scholar at Columbia University in New York.

His compositions have been selected for performance at major festivals such as ISCM, SEA-MUS, and ICMC. As a music theorist, he has read papers at many professional conferences such as ICMPC, SMPC, and ICMC.

He studied music theory with Jonathan D. Kramer and Joseph Dubiel, computer music with Brad Garton and Mara Helmuth, and composition with Masayuki Nagatomi and Kazumi Yanai. He received a BA and an MA in philosophy from Keio University in Tokyo, and an MA, an MPhil, and a PhD in music from Columbia University. http://music.columbia.edu/-akira/

It may be unfair to label **Jesper Holmen**'s music with his own term 'Chamber Punk' because, as all labels, it only accentuate certain aspects of certain works and not the variety of it all. It does, however, make sense to begin with this term, as it seems capable of describing some essential impulses in Holmen's aesthetics. His approach to composing for classical instruments seems to be infused with the energy of punk and postpunk rock music – an energy based on brutal, ecstatic, noisy and abrasive impulses.
A common denominator in Holmen's works is a gesture in which everything seems to slither askew. It sounds like microtonal glissandi within a cluster harmonic, even though the effect is often achieved without actual, notated glissandi, but by side effects of pushing the instruments to their limits, impeding tonal precision. Much of the intensity of Holmen's music lies in these slithering frictions.

Panayiotis Kokoras studied composition with I.Ioannidi, K. Varotsi, A. Kergomard and classical guitar with E. Asimakopoulo in Athens, Greece. In 1999 he moved to England, for postgraduate studies where he completed his MA and PhD in composition with T. Myatt at the University of York with funds from Arts and Humanities Research Board (AHRB) and Aleksandra Trianti Music Scholarships (Society Friends of Music) among others.

His works have been commissioned by institutes and festivals such as FROMM (Harvard University) IRCAM, MATA (Music At The Anthology), Spring Festival (The University of York), Gaudeamus (Netherlands), and regularly performed in international festivals and concert series throughout Europe, Asia and America. His compositions have received 31 distinctions and prizes in international competitions among others Bourges 2008 and 2004 – France, Gianni Bergamo 2007 – Switzerland, Pierre Schaeffer 2005 - Italy, Musica Viva 2005 and 2002 - Portugal, Look and Listen Prize 2004 - New York, Gaudeamus 2004 and 2003 – The Netherlands, Insulae Electronicae 2003 - Italy, Jurgenson Competition 2003 - Russia, Seoul international competition 2003 - Korea, Takemitsu Composition Award 2002 - Japan, Noroit Prize 2002 - France, CIMESP 2002 - Brazil, Musica Nova 2001 – Czech Republic, Métamorphoses 2000 - Belgium. Moreover, they have been selected by juries at more than 100 international call for scores opportunities and performed in over 70 cities around the world. www.panayiotiskokoras.com

Alex Harker composes electroacoustic, instrumental and interactive music. His most recent work focuses on strategies for bringing together these sometimes disparate fields to create an engaging and coherent whole.

He first studied composition formally with Gwyn Pritchard in Bristol and has since had numerous composition teacher, including Vic Hoyland, Jonty Harrison, Eric Oña, David

Berezan and Scott Wilson. In October 2006 he moved to York to start his PhD study with Ambrose Field and Roger Marsh. His PhD study was funded by the Arts and Humanities Research Council. He is currently a Research Fellow at the University of Huddersfield, working both as a composer, and also as a developer for the HISSTools project.
His works have been performed and workshopped in the UK, France and Switzerland by the Worldscape Laptop Orchestra, Darragh Morgan, Elastic Axis, BEAST, the University of Birmingham New Music Ensemble and Birmingham Contemporary Music Group.

He is also active as a performer of contemporary music in the roles of conductor and laptop performer.

João Pedro Oliveira is one of the most prominent Portuguese composers of his generation. He studied organ performance and composition and completed a PhD in Music at the University of New York at Stony Brook. His music includes one chamber opera, several orchestral composition, a Requiem, 3 string quartets, chamber music, solo instrumental music and electroacoustic music. He has received numerous prizes and awards, including three Prizes at Bourges Electroacoustic Music Competition, the prestigious Magisterium Prize in the same competition, the Giga-Hertz Special Award, 1st Prize in Metamorphoses competition, 1st Prize in Yamaha-Visiones Sonoras Competition, 1st Prize in Musica Nova competition, etc.. He is Professor at Federal University of Minas Gerais (Brazil) and Aveiro University (Portugal) and teaches composition, electroacoustic music and analysis. He published several articles in journals, and has written a book about analysis and 20th century music theory.

Concert 2

Atau Tanaka Atau Tanaka's first influences came from meeting John Cage at the Norton Lectures, and would go on to recreate Cage's Variations VII. Atau formed Sensorband with Zbigniew Karkowski and Edwin van der Heide in the 90's. He has releases on labels such as Sub Rosa, Bip-hop, Touch/Ash, Sonoris. He has been artistic co-director of STEIM, and director of Culture Lab, his work has been presented at Ars Electronica, ZKM, Sonar Festival. He is currently based in London at Goldsmiths, University of London.

Adam Parkinson is an electronic musician based in Newcastle, England. He has recently completed PhD, with much of his research looking at mobile music and performing with iPhones. He has worked alongside various improvisers such as Rhodri Davies, Klaus Filip, Robin Hayward and Dominic Lash, and has been involved in collaborations to create sound installations with Kaffe Matthews and Caroline Bergvall. He also dabbles in making dance music, and is trying to write a perfect pop song.

Yuta Uozumi Faculty of Media Science,Tokyo University of Technology, Japan.
A sound artist and agent-based composer was born in the suburbs of Osaka, Japan. He started computer music at the age of fifteen. He received his Ph.D. from Keio University SFC Graduate School of Media and Governance. He is researching Multi-Agent based dynamic composition with computer or human ensembles as a lecturer in Tokyo University of

Technology.

Works: In 2002 His CD "meme?" was released from Cubicmusic Japan (under the name of SamuraiJazz). In 2003 agent-based musical interface "Chase" was accepted by NIME (International Conference on New Interfaces for Musical Expression), it is a collaborative project by system-designer, DSP engineer and performer. In 2005 an application for agent-based composition "Gismo" and a piece created with the system "Chain" (early version) were accepted by ICMC(International Computer Music Conference), and more.

Dan Tramte is currently working towards his PhD in music composition with a specialization in computer music media at the University of North Texas. He also holds degrees in percussion performance (BM) and Composition (MM) from Bowling Green State University (Ohio). His primary teachers have included Elainie Lillios, Mikel Kuehn, Jon Nelson, Andrew May, and David Bithell. At North Texas, Dan Tramte serves as a graduate assistant for the Center for Experimental Music and Intermedia (CEMI); he also teaches Beginning/Class Composition (MUCP 1180/3080). His music has been programmed on numerous computer music conferences and can be heard on the CDCM computer music series, vol. 38.

Dimitri Paile is a musician and sound designer from Helsinki. This is his story. "Horoshi Marozhi! Horoshi Marozhi! ", people's ears would often seem to pick up. It was the strange sales-pitch of Nikolai, the Russian-speaking orphan who would sell ice-cream on the streets of Helsinki in the 1920's. In another part of town the young, talented pianist Asta Westzynthius was quickly learning and performing Chopin's finest on the grand piano. Asta and Nikolai knew nothing of each other until their children met at a school ball in the flower-decade. Despite different backgrounds, both Wendla and Alexander went to study medicine. Playing doctor soon resulted in four children. Young Dimitri grew up learning music from Asta and creative thinking from Nikolai. Dimitri quickly discovered his only true love to be music. Today he has played various instruments in underground punk bands, and made music and sound design for old and new media. http://dimitripaile.com

Butch Rovan is a composer/performer at Brown University, where he co-directs MEME (Multimedia & Electronic Music Experiments). Prior to joining Brown he directed CEMI at the University of North Texas, and was a compositeur en recherche at IRCAM. Rovan has received prizes from the Bourges International Electroacoustic Music Competition, the Berlin Transmediale International Media Arts Festival, and his work has been performed throughout Europe and the U.S. His research has been featured in Trends in Gestural Control of Music (IRCAM 2000), and appears in the book Mapping Landscapes for Performance as Research: Scholarly Acts and Creative Cartographies (Palgrave Macmillan 2009).

Lucky Leone is a professional artist whose work ranges from Sculpture to Painting to Video to works that use elements from all three disciplines. Lucky employs humor is almost all of his work, and is especially interested in pieces that work on many levels. Lucky Leone received a BFA and an MFA from the Rhode Island School of Design and an MFA from San Diego State University. Lucky has exhibited widely, mostly in academic galleries and museums. Lucky has taught Sculpture, Three-Dimensional Design, Drawing, Life Drawing, Freshman and Sophomore Seminars, and some other classes that he cannot remember at the Rhode Island School of Design, Bristol Community College (MA), San Diego State University (CA), The School of the Boston Museum of Fine Arts (MA), and Brown University (RI).

Sound Installations

Martin Rumori was born 1976 in Berlin. He studied musicology, computer science and philosophy. In 2005, he received his M.A. in musicology and computer science. From 2005–2010 he worked in Klanglabor (sound laboratory) at Academy of Media Arts Cologne (Germany), where he taught sound art, media composition, acoustics and sound engineering. Since 2011, he holds a position within the research project The Choreography of Sound at Institute of Electronic Music and Acoustics Graz (Austria). Martin is a Ph.D. student at the same institute with instructor Gerhard Eckel.

Martin's artistic work currently focuses on binaural technology for audio augmented environments, everyday life narration, poetic and anecdotic auditive surroundings, field recordings and phonography, advanced spatial projection techniques and algorithmic sound composition. He advocates the use of open source software and investigates its effects on the artistic creation process.

Peter Batchelor is a composer and sound artist living in Birmingham, UK. He has studied with Jonty Harrison and Andrew Lewis and is currently a lecturer at De Montfort University, Leicester. Predominantly working with fixed-media, his output ranges from two-channel 'tape' compositions for concert diffusion to large-scale multi-channel installation work.

Laura Maes (1978, Ghent, Belgium) completed her 'Master in Music' at the 'Royal Conservatory' in Ghent in 2001 with high distinction. In 2002 she received her Masters in Marketing Management with distinction at the Vlerick Leuven Gent Management School.

She is currently working as a researcher at the School of Arts of the University College Ghent, Faculty of Music, where she pursues her PhD in the arts under the supervision of Dr. Godfried-Willem Raes and Prof. Dr. Marc Leman. Her dissertation subject is sound art.

She has presented sound works in Belgium and abroad and is active as a musician in various ensembles. She performed together with, amongst others, Nico Parlevliet, Roel Meelkop, Claus Van Bebber, Noise-Maker's Fifes, Pierre Berthet, Logos Foundation, Q-O2 & Black Jackets Company and released records on C.U.E. records, Cling Film, MSBR-records, Denshi Zatsuon & Flenix.

Ted Apel is a sound artist whose sculptures and installations focus on the audio transducing element as the source of visual and sonic material.
He has exhibited his work at sound art festivals and exhibits including the SoundCulture

festival in San Francisco; the Ussachevsky Festival in Claremont, California; the Audio Art Festival in Krakow, Poland; the Sound Symposium in St. John's Newfoundland. the O.K. Center for Contemporary Art in Linz, Austria, and the Academy of Arts, Berlin.

He was twice a prizewinner at the Bourges International Electroacoustic Music Competition for his sound installations; his sound installation received an honorary mention at the Prix Ars Electronica 2001; and won the grand prize in the 2004 Idaho Triennial.

Ted Apel received his M.A. in electroacoustic music at Dartmouth College and his Ph.D. in computer music at the University of California, San Diego. He is currently teaching computer music and new media art as adjunct faculty at Boise State University.

Having finished his MA in Sonic Art last year at SARC, Queen's University Belfast, **James Nesfield** is currently a doctoral researcher in Aalto University's Media Lab as a member of the Sound and Physical Interaction research group [SOPI]. His research combines embodied and enactive frameworks, HCI and sonic interaction design. Artistically, his main areas of interest encompass and mix sonification, multimodal physicality and auditory perception. See james.nesfield.org for previous and current projects.

Concert 3

Peter Van Zandt Lane (b. 1985) is an American composer living in the Boston area, and has written music for a variety of ensembles across the country and beyond. His music often engages technology and its influence on art music in the 20th and 21st centuries through the use of live electronics and/or fixed media. Drawing inspiration from neo-classical, modernist, jazz, rock, electronica, and early music, he draws on his diverse experiences to compose music that is fresh, genuine, and engaging. He has recently been commissioned by the Barlow Endowment for the Quux Collective, the Wellesley Composers Conference and Chamber Music Center, and the SUNY Purchase Percussion Ensemble, among others. As a bassoonist he has premiered dozens of new works by living composers, often highlighting the bassoon as a versatile instrument in an electroacoustic setting. Peter is currently completing his PhD in Music Composition and Theory at Brandeis University.

Arne Eigenfeldt is a composer of live electroacoustic music, and a researcher into intelligent generative music systems. His music has been performed around the world, and his collaborations range from Persian Tar masters to contemporary dance companies to musical robots. He is currently an associate professor of music and technology at Simon Fraser University, Canada, and is the co-director of the Musical MetaCreation research group (metacreation.net), which aims to endow computers with creative behaviour. His research into intelligent musical agents has been presented at conferences such as ICMC, NIME, SEAMUS, ISMIR, EMS, SMC, EvoMusArt and ICCC, while the artistic output of his systems have been shown at ICMC, SEAMUS, SMC, and Generative Arts.

Shawn Trail has concentrated on musical robotics intimately for the past five years, realizing specific systems for improvisation and new performance contexts for musical robotics and novel control interfaces. In 2008 he was composer- in-residence with LEMUR (League of Electronic Musical Urban Robots) resulting in a concert featuring his multi- instrumental improviser's collective, Development. This iteration included processed tenor saxophone (Tony Barba), Xylosynth (Trail), visuals (John Cason) and the LEMUR instruments. During 2009-2010 Trail was a Fulbright Scholar at Medialogy, Aalborg University Copenhagen pursuing pitched percussion interface solutions for performance. This led to a position as Robotic and Control Interface Technician for Pat Metheny's Orchestrion Tour and subsequent HD-3D video production. Currently Trail is an Interdisciplinary PhD student in Computer Science, Electrical Engineering, and Music at the University of Victoria with supervisors George Tzanetakis, Peter Driessen, and Andrew Schloss. His research is concerned with extending traditional and conventional acoustic pitched percussion instruments using gesture recognition that utilizes sensor technologies, music information retrieval, and machine learning focused on non-invasive interface solutions incorporating computer vision and DSP. Involved in the design and fabrication of custom synthesis and robotic instruments, Trail also develops their gestural language, repertoire, and performance contexts collaboratively with the members of his research group. His multi-media performance works singularly revolve around minimal, textural evolving polyrhythmic, melodic ostinati propelled by a sense of urgency intrinsic to cultural music rituals informed by ancient traditions.

Scott Miller is a composer of electroacoustic, orchestral, chamber, choral and multimedia works frequently performed at venues and in exhibitions throughout North America and Europe, including the 10th International Music Festival New Music Plus in Brno, The Contemporary Music Festival at the Ostrava Creative Center and Janácek Conservatory, Mladé Pódium International Festival of Young Artists, the 12th International Festival of Electroacoustic Music in Brno, the Leipzig Neue Gewandhaus, at Dvorak Hall, Prague, and at Galerie EXPRMNTL, in Toulouse, France. Miller's music has been described as 'peaceful, intimate, and painstakingly crafted' (Christy Desmith, City Pages) and 'not for the faint-hearted listener; it is tough, unsparing, blessed free of self-indulgence and offering for our consolation only its scrupulous precision.' (Juliet Patterson, mnartists.org).

Nick Collins is a composer, performer and researcher, with interests including machine listening, interactive and generative music, and audiovisuals. He co-edited the Cambridge Companion to Electronic Music (Cambridge University Press 2007) and The SuperCollider Book (MIT Press, 2011) and wrote the Introduction to Computer Music (Wiley 2009). iPhone apps include RISCy, Concat, BBCut and VideoNoise. Notable concerts include live coding in a vineyard in Corfu, falling off a piano stool in Sydney, and singing the 100 metres in Brighton. Sometimes, he writes in the third person about himself, but is trying to give it up. Further details, including publications, music, code and more, are available from http://www.sussex.ac.uk/Users/nc81/index.html

Steven Kemper composes music for acoustic instruments, instruments and computers, musical robots, dance, video, and networked systems. He is currently a Ph.D. candidate at the University of Virginia in Composition and Computer Technologies. Steven's works have been presented at ICMC, SEAMUS, SIGCHI, FEMF, Pixilerations, American Composers Alliance Festival of American Music, and the Seoul International Computer Music Festival. In 2010, Steven won the International Computer Music Association 2010 Student Award for Best Submission for Shadows no. 5, part of a collaborative series of pieces with composer and dancer Aurie Hsu, for tribal fusion belly dance, electroacoustic music and RAKS (Remote electroAcoustic Kinesthetic Sensing) System, a wireless sensor interface designed specifically for tribal fusion belly dancer. Steven is a co-founder of Expressive Machines Musical Instruments, and a member of UVA's Interactive Media Research Group (IMRG) where he is a software developer for NOMADS (Network-Operational Mobile Applied Digital System), a web based tool for artistic creation and teaching in large-scale classroom and performance contexts.

Troy Rogers is a composer/instrument designer whose primary research interest lies in the realm of musical robotics. He is currently a Ph.D. student at the University of Virginia, completing a degree in Composition and Computer Technologies. At the University of Virginia, he teamed up with fellow composers Steven Kemper and Scott Barton to form Expressive Machines Musical Instruments (EMMI), a group dedicated to the creation and musical exploration of robotic musical instruments. As a 2009-10 Fulbright Research Fellow, Troy spent time at the Logos Foundation in Ghent, Belgium where he apprenticed with Godfried-Willem Raes, creator of the Man and Machine Robot Orchestra. Troy's output also includes music for soloists, chamber ensembles, orchestra, dance, theater, and digital media. He has spent time as a composer/researcher at Simon Fraser University's Sonic Research Studio exploring acoustic ecology and soundscape composition, and at the University of Oregon's Cognitive Modeling and Eye Tracking Laboratory creating audio/visual art controlled by eye movements. More recently he has worked with architects Jason Johnson and Nataly Gattegno of Future Cities Lab on projects exploring the intersection of kinetic, interactive architecture and musical robotics.

Scott Barton is a composer, guitarist and recordist currently pursuing his Ph.D. in the Composition and Computer Technologies program at the University of Virginia. His current interests include: rhythmic complexity, auditory and temporal perception, musical robots, audio engineering and rock music. He is currently working on a dissertation that explores the cognitive and contextual inputs to musical discontinuity perception. He co-founded Expressive Machines Musical Instruments (EMMI), a collective focused on designing and building robotic musical instruments (www.expressivemachines.com), with Troy Rogers and Steven Kemper. He studied music and philosophy at Colgate University and received his Master of Music in Composition from the Brooklyn College Conservatory of Music. Important influence upon Scott's music and thought have come by way of Jonathan Schlackman, Jordan Berk, Dexter Morrill, Tania Leon, Rory Stuart, Amnon Wolman, Judith Shatin, Matthew Burtner and Ted Coffey.

Performers

Born in Canada, clarinetist **Heather Roche** trained in England and now lives in Cologne, Germany. She has performed at some of the major European festivals, including musik-Fest (Berlin), BachFest (Leipzig), Musica Nova (Helsinki), the Huddersfield Contemporary Music Festival, Acht Brücken (Cologne), the International Computer Music Conference, the Wittener Tage für Neue Kammermusik and the Agora Festival (Ircam, Paris). She is a member of the ensemble hand werk (Cologne). She holds a PhD from the University of Huddersfield and a Masters of Music from the Guildhall School of Music and Drama (London).

About FIGURA

A mezzo-soprano, three musicians, a composer, a poet and an architect – **FIGURA Ensemble** is a musical collective with a mind of its own.
Each of the seven artists of FIGURA are among Denmark's most respected – Helene Gjerris, Jesper Egelund, Frans Hansen, Anna Klett, Peter Bruun, Filippa Berglund and Ursula Andkjær Olsen.
Together, over the last 19 years, FIGURA has challenged both collaborators and audiences alike with exceptional concerts and modern music theatre – not to mention their 'Small Composers' workshops that reach out to the coming generation of music-lovers.

FIGURA'S RECENT AWARDS AND NOMINATIONS

2011: FIGURA's 'Small Composers' education project awarded the YEAH! Young EARopean Award
2010: Helene Gjerris awarded the Danish Composer's Society's Musician Prize
2009: The Reumert Prize for Best Children's Theatre of the Year for 'The Story of a Mother' / Ursula Andkjær Olsen nominated for Nordic Council Literature Prize 2009 and awarded the National Arts Foundation Literature Committee Prize for 'Havet er en scene' (The Ocean is a Stage)
2008: Peter Bruun awarded the Nordic Council Music Prize for the opera 'Miki Alone' with libretto by Ursula Andkjær Olsen.

Signe Asmussen (voice)

Since graduating from the Royal Academy of Music in Copenhagen with reviews that named her "the voice of possibilities", "a natural interpreter", and "an intimate vocal-seducer", Danish soprano Signe Asmussen has worked as a soloist with most of the national orchestras and choirs.

Now, she is one of the most sought-after, Danish recitalists, with an ongoing cooperation with pianists such as Christen Stubbe Teglbjærg, Christian Westergaard, Erik Kaltoft, and Norwegian Arne Jørgen Fæø, promoting one of her favourite disciplines: The intimate recital with focus on the extended lied-repertoire from all around the world, which brings her in close contact with her audience. For this, she has recently been awarded the prestigious Aksel Schiøtz Prize 2009.

She has worked with international renowned conductors and pianists such as Michel Tabachnik, Franck Ollu, Lan Shui, Lars Ulrik Mortensen, Rodolfo Fischer, Michael Seal, Alexander and Howard Shelley, Peter Hill, and Rudolf Jansen, and international concert venues count Wigmore Hall and National Gallery in London, Symphony Hall in Birmingham, The National Galleries in Edinburgh, Concertgebouw in Amsterdam, along with all of the important concert halls in DK.
She has appeared in numerous productions at the Royal Opera, Copenhagen, and The National Opera, Århus: as Cherubino in "Le Nozze di Figaro", Bertha in "Il Barbiere di Siviglia", Valencienne in "The Merry Widow", Suzuki in "Madama Butterfly", and recently as a very successfull Idamante in "Idomeneo", as well as Musette in "La Bohème".

Anna Klett (clarinetist)
Faroese clarinetist, studied at the Royal Danish Academy of Music in Copenhagen at Jørgen Misser and Bent Neuchs debut in 1994 and that same year Premier Prix from Conservatoire the Musique de Geneve at Thomas Friedli.
She has worked with many orchestras and ensembles in Denmark but with great love, devoted most of her time to contemporary music. Anna Klett is a member of FIGURA and Athelas Sinfonietta and is cofounder of the Faroese chamber ensemble Aldubáran.
Anna Klett has received the Danish Composer's Society of Musicians's Prize 2002 and the Danish Music Critics Award 2003.

Frans Hansen (percussionist)
was educated at the Royal Academy of Music in Copenhagen and debuted in 1983. He has since been active at the stage of contemporary music in Denmark as a member of ensembles such as the Elsinore Players, Danish Piano Theatre, Touché, Tuku-tukahh ..., Aarhus Sinfonietta and FIGURA.
Frans Hansen has participated in numerous performances of works in the genre of "instrumental theater" - especially the works of Mauricio Kagel. He has previously taught percussion at both the Royal Academy of Music and Funen and Northern Jutland Academy of Music.

Jesper Egelund (bassist, ensemble director)
In collaboration with Helene Gjerris - founder of FIGURA Ensemble in 1993.
Educated at the Royal Danish Academy of Music and VSMU (Music Academy) in Bratislava. 1988-89 he was selected for the Gustav Mahler Youth Orchestra (chief conductor Claudio Abbado). Have besides 5 years in the Danish Radio Sinfonietta since his graduation in 1993, primarily been a freelancer and starred in a series of performances including The last Virtuoso, Den Anden Opera 1995, Black Rider, Betty Nansen 1998, Hamlet, Det Lille Turnéteater 1998, The story of the little uncle, Theater La Balance 2000, On this Planet, Kaleidoscope / Den Anden Opera 2002, Miki Alone, Simsalabad, Den Anden Opera 2005
Jesper has an extensive work as a composer among others on: The Road to my Father and

King UBU, Corona La Balance 2007. He has been touring in the U.S., Russia, Korea, Scotland, Scandinavia, Germany, Canada, Greenland and Japan. He is also a member of the Quartet in 4 Elements.